Bus Handbook

April 1994

British Bus Publishing

The South Midlands Bus Handbook

The South Midlands Bus Handbook is part of the Bus Handbook series that details the fleets of stage carriage and express coach operators. Where space allows other significant operators in the areas covered are also included. These handbooks are published by British Bus Publishing and cover Scotland, Wales and England north of London. Companion volumes, The Yorkshire Bus Handbook, The Eastern Bus Handbook, The North East Bus Handbook and The North Midlands Bus Handbook, are currently available. Handbooks for East Midlands, Wales, the North West and Scotland are also planned for 1994. Together with the London Bus Handbooks, South East Buses and South West Buses published by Capital Transport, they provide comprehensive coverage of all the principal operators' fleets in the British Isles.

Quality photographs for inclusion in these, and other areas covered by the series are welcome, though the publishers cannot accept responsibility for any loss. Details of changes to fleet information are also welcome.

More information on the Bus Handbook series is available from:

British Bus Publishing,
The Vyne,
16 St Margaret's Drive
Wellington
Telford,
Shropshire TF1 3PH

Series Editor: Bill Potter
Principal Editors for The South Midlands Bus Handbook:
Bill Potter, David Donati and Alan Mills

Acknowledgements:
We are grateful to Keith Grimes, Mark Jameson, Tony Hunter, Ken Jubb,
Colin Lloyd, Geoff Mills, Steve Sanderson, the PSV Circle and the operating
companies for their assistance in the compilation of this book.

The front cover photo is by Bill Potter
The rear cover and frontispiece photographs are by Ken Jubb, Clive Beeton and Brian Pritchard.

Contents correct to April 1994

ISBN 1 897990 05 7
Published by British Bus Publishing
The Vyne, 16 St Margarets Drive, Wellington,
Telford, Shropshire, TF1 3PH
© British Bus Publishing, April 1994

Contents

ASTONS

Astons of Kempsey (Coaches) Ltd, 4 Church Street, Kempsey,
Hereford & Worcester, WR5 3JG
TW & SD Halford, 4 Church Street, Kempsey, Hereford & Worcester, WR5 3JG

HJI531	Volvo B58-56	Plaxton Elite III	C53F	1972	Ex Bennetts, Gloucester, 1989
DSU114	Volvo B58-56	Plaxton P'mount 3200 (1986)	C53F	1973	Ex Pullman, Penclawdd, 1992
IIB696	Volvo B58-61	Plaxton Elite III	C53F	1974	Ex Ashton, Lisburn, 1988
GGD664T	Volvo B58-61	Plaxton Supreme IV	C57F	1979	Ex Pykett, Kilburn, 1989
NIA5055	Volvo B58-61	Plaxton Supreme IV	C57F	1980	Ex Thandi, Smethwick, 1989
267ALP	Auwaerter Neoplan N126H	Auwaerter Jetliner	C49FT	1982	Ex Beavis, Bussage, 1993
A676EYJ	Mercedes-Benz L508D	Mercedes-Benz	M14	1984	Acquired 1992
IIB145	Volvo B10M-61	Jonckheere Jubilee P50	C49F	1985	
HYY3	Volvo B10M-61	Jonckheere Jubilee P50	C57F	1985	Ex Buddens, Woodfalls, 1988
RDU4	Volvo B10M-61	Plaxton Paramount 3500 II	C49F	1986	Ex Kime, Folkingham, 1991
A1FRP	Volvo B10M-61	Plaxton Paramount 3500 III	C57F	1987	Ex Trathens, Plymouth, 1991
3698E	Scania K112TRS	Plaxton Paramount 4000	CH55/20DT	1987	Ex Ementon, Cranfield, 1988
24PAE	Scania K112CRB	Plaxton Paramount 3500 III	C49FT	1988	Ex Mercury Incentive, Horley, 1990
PJI2403	Volvo B10M-61	Caetano Algarve	C49FT	1988	Acquired 1993
F112TEE	Mercedes-Benz 507D	Coachcraft	M10L	1989	Ex B&D Richards, Cimla, 1993
G490PNF	Mercedes-Benz 508D	Made-to-Measure	C20F	1989	Ex Berry, Stockton, 1993
G577RNC	Peugeot-Talbot Express	Made-to-Measure	M11	1989	
G400CVC	Volvo B10M-50	Van Hool Alizée	C49FT	1990	Ex Harry Shaw, Coventry, 1993
G230HNP	Bova FHD12.290	Bova Futura	C51F	1990	
H726UKY	Ford Transit VE6	Advanced Vehicle Bodies	M12	1991	Ex Kenning Car Hire, 1993
H170NHP	Volvo B10M-50	Jonckheere Deauville P599	C53FT	1991	Ex Harry Shaw, Coventry, 1994
J336UHP	Peugeot-Talbot Express	Talbot	M8	1992	
L614CPM	Dennis Javelin 12SDA2125	Plaxton Première 350	C53FT	1993	Ex Dennis demonstrator, 1994
L360YNR	Dennis Javelin 12SDA2125	Plaxton Première 350	C53FT	1994	
L230BUT	Dennis Javelin 12SDA2125	Plaxton Premiére 350	C53FT	1994	

Previous Registrations:

24PAE	E585OEF	HYY3	C405LRP
267ALP	KVJ1Y	IIB145	B968CWP, RDU4, B262MAB
3698E	From new	IIB696	RBD76M
A1FRP	D874EEH	NIA5055	GJU855V
DSU114	JWO946L	PIJ2403	?
H170NHP	H5URE	RDU4	D111HMH
HJI531	XWX797L		

Livery: White, grey and brown; Dark grey (coaches)

Opposite, top: **Ludlows is based in Halesowen, and ORP466M is seen here in Halesowen Bus Station on the Romsley service. This Leyland National has been in the Ludlow fleet for six years since arriving from United Counties in 1988.** *Phillip Stephenson*

Oppostite, bottom: **Guide Friday operates mainly open top double deckers, but has two open top single deckers, both 1947 AEC Regals. One of these often operates the Cotswold Tour from Stratford. The 'inclement weather' vehicle is, however, photographed here. CHL772 is a good example of early post-war Willowbrook-bodied vehicles - this one on Daimler CVD6 chassis was new to Bullock, Wakefield but came to Guide Friday in 1989 from Hastings.** *Tim Weatherup*

One of the oldest vehicles in the Astons fleet is GGD664T. This Plaxton-bodied Volvo B58 was new in February 1979, but did not come to Astons until 1989. Originally a 50 seater, it was fitted with 57 seats by Astons. *Richard Eversden*

Astons contract a number of vehicles to companies specialising in ski-ing holidays, and these, in some cases, carry permanent Ski-Astons legends with a different livery. G400CVC, here retaining its former owners' livery, is one of the tri-axle Volvo B10M-50 models with Van Hool bodywork. These are increasingly favoured by some operators to overcome axle-weight problems in the UK where regulations are currently more stringent than on the continent. *Colin Lloyd*

BANGA TRAVEL

Parkash R Banga, 4 Vicarage Road, Wolverhampton, West Midlands, WV2 1DT

	D31SAO	Renault-Dodge S56	Reeve Burgess	B23F	1986	Ex Cumberland, 1994
B2	D528NDA	Freight Rover Sherpa	Carlyle	B19F	1986	Ex Williams, Runcord, 1993
	D69OKG	Freight Rover Sherpa	Carlyle	B18F	1987	Ex Delivered-in-Style, Syston, 1993
	D190NON	Freight Rover Sherpa	Carlyle	B18F	1987	Ex MCH, Uxbridge, 1993
	E403EPE	Renault-Dodge S46	Northern Counties	B22F	1987	Ex Stagecoach South, 1993
B4	E410EPE	Renault-Dodge S46	Northern Counties	B22F	1987	Ex Stagecoach South, 1993

Livery: Cream and blue

Banga Travel of Wolverhampton operate D528NDA a Carlyle-bodied Freight Rover formerly with, West Midlands Travel, on their main service 77 from Wolverhampton to Rocket Pool. *Roy Marshall*

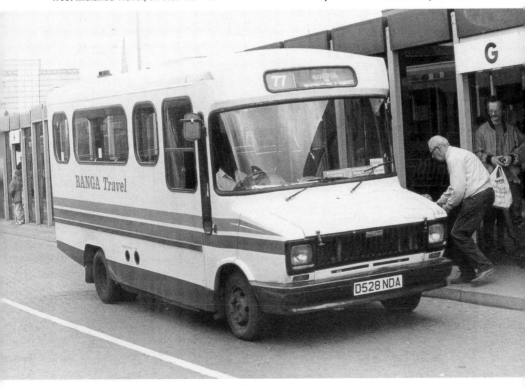

BILL MORRIS

C G Morris, Broadbridge House, Stourport Road, Bromyard,
Hereford & Worcester, HR7 4NT

ADC177A	Bedford YMT	Duple Dominant II	C30FT	1979	Ex Travel G's Way, Mancot, 1994
AVJ600V	Volvo B58-56	Plaxton Supreme IV Express	C53F	1980	
EJX355V	Volvo B58-61	Plaxton Supreme IV	C51F	1980	Ex Stretton Travel, Cardington, 1994
JKL642Y	MCW Metroliner CR126/2	MCW	C51F	1983	Ex Dunn-Line, Nottingham, 1993
A260BTY	Leyland Royal Tiger B50	Roe Doyen	C51F	1984	Ex Westbus, Ashford, 1991

Previous Registrations:

ADC177A	ENS345T		JKL642Y	FKK844Y, PFN873
EJX355V	LUA241V, 496WNN			

Livery: Blue and/or white

Rather unusual for a small country independent, Bill Morris of Bromyard has this erstwhile East Kent MCW Metroliner, JKL642Y. It is seen in Bromyard at the end of March 1994 while heading for Worcester on service 425. *Martin Perry*

THE BIRMINGHAM COACH COMPANY

Birmingham Omnibus Co Ltd, Cross Keys Bus Park, Hallbridge Way, Tipton Road
Tividale, West Midlands, B69 3MY

	Reg	Chassis	Body	Seating	Year	History
	222UPD	Leyland Leopard PSU3D/4R	Duple 320(1988)	C53F	1977	Ex Alexander, Sheffield, 1986
	AAL272A	Leyland Leopard PSU5D/4R	Plaxton P'mount 3200(1987)	C53F	1980	Ex National Welsh, 1992
	AAL345A	Leyland Leopard PSU5D/4R	Plaxton P'mount 3200(1987)	C53F	1980	Ex National Welsh, 1992
	AAL453A	Leyland Leopard PSU5D/4R	Plaxton P'mount 3200(1987)	C53F	1980	Ex National Welsh, 1992
	CSU993	Leyland Leopard PSU5C/4R	Plaxton Supreme V	C53F	1982	Ex Wessex, 1990
	YSV739	Leyland Leopard PSU5C/4R	Plaxton Supreme V	C53F	1982	Ex Wessex, 1990
	XXI8563	Scania K112CRS	Jonckheere Jubilee P599	C51FT	1984	Ex Transcity, Sidcup, 1991
	SIB8342	Volvo B10M-61	Van Hool Alizée	C49FT	1985	Ex Cambridge Coach Services, 1991
	SIB8341	Scania K112CRS	Van Hool Alizée	C49FT	1985	Ex Westerham Coaches, 1992
	SIB8340	DAF SB2300DHS585	Jonckheere Jubilee P599	C28FT	1986	Ex Lucking, Washington, 1991
	J4BCC	Mercedes-Benz 609D	Made-to-Measure	C24F	1991	
	L4BCC	Volvo B10M-60	Plaxton Excalibur	C49F	1993	
2	KSO76P	Leyland National 10351/2R		B40D	1976	Ex Trefaldwyn, Montgomery, 1988
3	GUG118N	Leyland National 11351/1R		B52F	1975	Ex PMT, 1989
4	HJA131N	Leyland National 10351/1R		B41F	1975	Ex Ludlows, Halesowen, 1990

AAL453A is one of three Leyland Leopard coaches acquired from Tellings-Golden Miller, Cardiff, which had spent most of their lives in the National Welsh fleet. The chassis date from 1980, but they were fitted with new Plaxton Paramount bodies and given new registrations in 1988. The Birmingham Coach Company had a contract for conveying theatregoers to the Alexandra Theatre in Birmingham - hence the advertising panel, which looks a little odd on a coach. *Tim Weatherup*

The staple vehicle in the Birmingham Coach Company fleet is the Leyland National. An early example 26, KOM789P, was new to West Midlands and has now returned to the area after a period with Shearings where it helped pioneer commercial stage services for that undertaking. *D Barber*

Coaches play a significant part in the operations of The Birmingham Coach Company. This DAF SB2300 with Jonckheere bodywork, SIB8340, has a very high specification for executive work - hence the Pullman logo on the side of the vehicle. *Tim Weatherup*

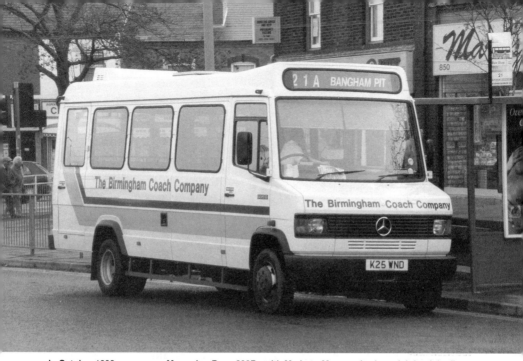

In October 1992, seven new Mercedes-Benz 609Ds with Made-to-Measure bodywork joined the fleet. K25WND is one of these vehicles, seen here on the City-Bangham Pit service. These would have been among the final year's production from the Manchester-based converter which started as Dixon-Lomas. *Tim Weatherup*

Vehicles have been acquired from several areas of the country to operate an extensive network of services in Birmingham and the Black Country. No.82, GMB650T, is a 10.3-metre vehicle which came from Crosville in 1993. *D Barber*

6	NOA199P	Leyland National 11351A/1R		B50F	1976	Ex Enterprise, Coventry, 1989
10	MTJ775S	Leyland National 11351A/1R		B52F	1976	Ex Merseybus, 1991
12	WYJ167S	Leyland National 11351A/2R		B44D	1978	Ex Brighton & Hove, 1992
14	GRM351L	Leyland National 1151/1R/0401		B52F	1973	Ex Cumberland, 1990
15	GRM353L	Leyland National 1151/1R/0401		B52F	1973	Ex Cumberland, 1990
16	GEU369N	Leyland National 10351/1R		B44F	1975	Ex Shearings, 1989
17	GEU371N	Leyland National 10351/1R		B44F	1975	Ex Shearings, 1989
19	HHU633N	Leyland National 10351/1R		B44F	1975	Ex Shearings, 1989
20	HHU634N	Leyland National 10351/1R		B44F	1975	Ex Shearings, 1989
22	GHU641N	Leyland National 10351/1R		B44F	1975	Ex Badgerline, 1986
23	BSF766S	Leyland National 11351A/1R		B52F	1978	Ex Western Scottish, 1991
25	RYG768R	Leyland National 11351A/2R		B52F	1976	Ex West Yorkshire, 1988
26	KOM789P	Leyland National 11351/2R		B46D	1976	Ex Shearings, 1989
27	KOM791P	Leyland National 11351/2R		B46D	1976	Ex Shearings, 1989
28	KOM793P	Leyland National 11351/2R		B46D	1976	Ex Shearings, 1989
30	NEL860M	Leyland National 1151/1R/2402		B49F	1974	Ex Shearings, 1989
31	MOD826P	Leyland National 11351A/1R		B50F	1976	Ex Shearings, 1990
33	YCW843N	Leyland National 10351/1R		B44F	1975	Ex Shearings, 1989
34	YCW845N	Leyland National 10351/1R		B44F	1975	Ex Badgerline, 1986
35	MOD850P	Leyland National 11351A/1R		B50F	1976	Ex Shearings, 1990
37	SKF18T	Leyland National 11351A/1R		B52F	1978	Ex Merseybus, 1991
40	EGB90T	Leyland National 11351A/1R		B52F	1978	Ex Western Scottish, 1991
41	EGB91T	Leyland National 11351A/1R		B52F	1978	Ex Western Scottish, 1991
44	SKF13T	Leyland National 11351A/1R		B49F	1978	Ex Merseybus, 1991
45	RKA873T	Leyland National 11351A/1R		B49F	1978	Ex Merseybus, 1991
46	RKA877T	Leyland National 11351A/1R		B49F	1978	Ex Merseybus, 1991
47	RKA878T	Leyland National 11351A/1R		B49F	1978	Ex Merseybus, 1991
48	RKA884T	Leyland National 11351A/1R		B49F	1978	Ex Merseybus, 1991
49	SKF20T	Leyland National 11351A/1R		B52F	1978	Ex Merseybus, 1991
50	SKF30T	Leyland National 11351A/1R		B52F	1978	Ex Merseybus, 1991
53	K29WND	Mercedes-Benz 609D	Made-to-Measure	B24F	1992	
54	K25WND	Mercedes-Benz 609D	Made-to-Measure	B24F	1992	
55	K28WND	Mercedes-Benz 609D	Made-to-Measure	B24F	1992	
56	YPF774T	Leyland National 10351A/1R		B41F	1978	Ex Brighton & Hove, 1992
58	K27WND	Mercedes-Benz 609D	Made-to-Measure	B24F	1992	
59	K26WND	Mercedes-Benz 609D	Made-to-Measure	B24F	1992	
60	K32WND	Mercedes-Benz 609D	Made-to-Measure	B24F	1992	
62	UFG55S	Leyland National 11351A/2R		B44D	1977	Ex Brighton & Hove, 1992
63	UFG55S	Leyland National 11351A/2R		B44D	1977	Ex Brighton & Hove, 1992
64	AYJ106T	Leyland National 11351A/1R		B52F	1978	Ex Brighton & Hove, 1992
65	YCD80T	Leyland National 11351A/2R		B44D	1978	Ex Brighton & Hove, 1992
66	UFG59S	Leyland National 11351A/1R		B44D	1977	Ex Brighton & Hove, 1992
67	WYJ166S	Leyland National 11351A/2R		B44D	1978	Ex Brighton & Hove, 1992
68	WPG224M	Leyland National 10351/1R/SC		DP39F	1974	Ex Reg's, Hertford, 1992
69	LPR940P	Leyland National 11351/1R		B49F	1976	Ex WMRCC, Swanley, 1992
71	HSC106T	Leyland National 11351A/1R		B49F	1978	Ex Fife Scottish, 1992
73	K31WND	Mercedes-Benz 609D	Made-to-Measure	B24F	1992	
74	YCD79T	Leyland National 11351A/2R		B44D	1978	Ex Brighton & Hove, 1992
75	AKU160T	Leyland National 10351B/1R		B44F	1979	Ex Black Prince, Morley, 1993
76	YYE291T	Leyland National 10351A/2R		B44F	1979	Ex Cyril Evans, Senghenydd, 1993
77	THX219S	Leyland National 10351A/2R		B44F	1978	Ex Cyril Evans, Senghenydd, 1993
78	OJD862R	Leyland National 10351A/2R		B44F	1977	Ex Cyril Evans, Senghenydd, 1993
79	HMA565T	Leyland National 10351B/1R		B44F	1978	Ex Kinch, Barrow-on-Soar, 1993
80	XAK451T	Leyland National 11351A/1R		B52F	1978	Ex Clyde Coast Services, 1993
81	GMB661T	Leyland National 10351B/1R		B44F	1978	Ex Kinch, Barrow-on-Soar, 1993
82	GMB650T	Leyland National 10351B/1R		B44F	1978	Ex Kinch, Barrow-on-Soar, 1993
83	PTF730L	Leyland National 1151/2R/0401		B52F	1972	Ex Ribble, 1993
84	NTC604M	Leyland National 1151/1R/0401		B49F	1973	Ex Ribble, 1993
85	JDZ4898	Auwaerter Neoplan N122/3	Auwaerter Skyliner	CH57/20DT	1985	Ex Trathens, Plymouth, 1993
86	UHG745R	Leyland National 11351A/1R		B49F	1977	Ex Ribble, 1993
87	SCK708P	Leyland National 11351A/1R		B49F	1977	Ex Ribble, 1993
	J413NCP	DAF SB220LC550	Ikarus Citibus	B48F	1992	Ex Hughes DAF demonstrator, 1994

Previous Registrations:

222UPD	VDH243S	CSU993	SND291X	SIB8341	D176PKE
AAL272A	BUH221V	JDZ4898	B668DVL	SIB8342	D848KVE
AAL345A	BUH220V	NOA199P	MOD824P, CSU993	XXI8563	A67JLW, C753TMY
AAL453A	BUH224V	SIB8340	D321VVV	YSV739	SND294X

Livery: Cream and red

BLUE LINE

K J & K J Wheadon, Units 24/6, Beech Business Park, Tillington Road,
Hereford, Hereford & Worcester, HR4 9QT

LAE894L	Bedford YRQ	Duple Viceroy	C45F	1973	Ex NCB, Edstaston, 1993
BCJ899V	Ford R1114	Plaxton Supreme IV	C53F	1980	Ex Golden Pioneer, Hereford, 1991
KRO656V	Ford R1114	Plaxton Supreme IV	C53F	1980	Ex Golden Pioneer, Hereford, 1991
LYB393Y	Bedford YMQ	Plaxton Paramount 3200	C31F	1983	Ex Otter Coaches, Ottery St Mary, 1994
D533MOK	Freight Rover Sherpa	Carlyle	B18F	1987	Ex Kenn Garage, Kenn, 1991
D883MWR	Freight Rover Sherpa	Dormobile	B20F	1987	Ex Owen's Motors, Knighton, 1992
D771PTU	Freight Rover Sherpa	Dormobile	B16F	1987	Ex Riverside Coaches, Telford, 1991
A3NPT	Bedford YNV Venturer	Caetano Algarve	C53F	1988	Ex National Plant & Transport, 1994
F377KVJ	Freight Rover Sherpa	Crystals	M16	1988	
F893MCJ	Freight Rover Sherpa	Freight Rover	M12	1989	

Previous Registrations:
A3NPT   E754JAY

Livery: White and blue

Leaving Halesowen bus station for Dudley is The Birmingham Coach Company's 66, UFG59S, another Leyland National, but one from Brighton & Hove. The livery carried in February 1994 shows much of the style used by this former operator. *Keith Grimes*

CARTERTON COACHES

J W Whitehead, 1 Brize Norton Road, Carterton, Oxfordshire, OX18 3HN

Depot: Black Bourton Road, Carterton

NNN11P	AEC Reliance 6U2R	Plaxton Supreme III Express	C53F	1976	Ex Carterton Coaches, 1992
NAL53P	Leyland Fleetline FE30AGR	Alexander AD	H44/34F	1976	Ex Carterton Coaches, 1992
OKW504R	Leyland Fleetline FE30AGR	MCW	H45/27D	1977	Ex Carterton Coaches, 1992
SDA620S	Leyland Fleetline FE30AGR	Park Royal	H43/33F	1977	Ex Carterton Coaches, 1992
NDD113W	Bedford YMT	Plaxton Supreme IV Express	C53F	1980	Ex Swanbrook, Cheltenham, 1993
XEL674X	MAN SR280H	MAN	C49FT	1982	Ex Pike, Smannell, 1993
RAD102R	DAF MB200DKFL600	Plaxton Paramount 3200	C51F	1983	Ex Carterton Coaches, 1992
GDZ8449	Scania K112CRS	Plaxton Paramount 3500	C49FT	1984	Ex Snell, Newton Abbot, 1993
A459JJF	Bova EL28/581	Bova Europa	C53F	1984	Ex Smith, Bold Heath, 1993
B112UTM	Scania K112CRS	Plaxton Paramount 3500	C53F	1984	Ex Gretton, Peterborough, 1993
C133CFB	MCW Metroliner DR130/24	MCW	CH57/22F	1986	Ex Waddon, Bedwas, 1992
C901JOF	MCW Metroliner DR130/30	MCW	CH57/15F	1986	Ex Central Coachways, 1993
C902JOF	MCW Metroliner DR130/30	MCW	CH47/17F	1986	Ex Central Coachways, 1993

Previous Registrations:

GDZ8449	A489POD	RAD102R	ANA457Y	XEL674X	STT618X, 5300RU

Livery: White, red and blue

Carterton is a residential community dominated by the near-by Brize Norton air base, and its in this area that the operator Carterton can be found. Photographed working the Saturday service to Norton is NNN11P, the only AEC and the last remaining example of the Plaxton Supreme III body in the fleet.
Bill Potter

CAVE

E H & G H Cave, 1-5 High Street, Solihull Lodge, Shirley, Solihull, West Midlands, B90 1JN

HHA126L	Leyland National 1151/1R/2501		B51F	1973	Ex Kirby, Wythall, 1991
GBF73N	Leyland National 11351/1R		B49F	1975	Ex PMT, 1992
YXI1760	Bedford YRQ	Duple Dominant	B36F	1976	Ex Waters, Wrexham, 1993
TTC534T	Leyland National 11351A/1R		B52F	1978	Ex Metrowest, Coseley, 1993
YPL397T	Leyland National 10351B/1R		B41F	1978	Ex D&G, Rachub, 1993
FCY280W	Bedford YMQ	Duple Dominant	DP45F	1980	Ex County Bus & Coach, 1993
FCY283W	Bedford YMQ	Duple Dominant	DP45F	1980	Ex County Bus & Coach, 1993
MKP181W	Bedford YMT	Wadham Stringer Vanguard	B61F	1981	Ex Boro'line Maidstone, 1987
J249SOC	Dennis Dart 9.8SDL3003	Carlyle Dartline	B40F	1991	
J921TUK	ACE Cougar	Willowbrook Warrior	B40F	1991	

Previous Registrations:
YXI1760   GHN857N

Livery: Turquoise and grey

One new service bus purchased by the Cave business is J249SOC, a Carlyle-bodied Dennis Dart, new in 1991. The service operated on this occasion goes a little further than the West Midlands County boundary to Hockley Heath. *D Barber*

CHARLTON SERVICES

NGJ, NHM & PD Holder, The Garage, High Street, Charlton-on-Otmoor, Oxfordshire, OX5 2UQ

GUD708L	Leyland Leopard PSU3B/4R	Plaxton Elite III	C51F	1972	
AAU136A	Leyland Leopard PSU5/4R	Plaxton Elite III	C57F	1973	Ex Lewis, Llanrhystyd, 1992
NWT637P	Leyland Leopard PSU3C/4R	Plaxton Supreme III	C46F	1976	Ex Kidlington Band, 1991
VGJ317R	Leyland Leopard PSU5A/4R	Plaxton Supreme III	C55F	1977	Ex Epsom Coaches, 1984
VPP958S	Leyland Leopard PSU5C/4R	Plaxton Supreme III	C57F	1978	Ex Biss Brothers, B Stortford, 1985
AFH190T	Leyland Leopard PSU5C/4R	Duple Dominant II	C50F	1978	Ex J & K, Kingswood, 1989
EDF269T	Leyland Leopard PSU5C/4R	Plaxton Supreme IV	C57F	1979	Ex Shamrock & Rambler, 1984
CSU432	Leyland Tiger TRCTL11/3R	Plaxton Supreme V	C53F	1982	Ex Raff, Gravesend, 1991
CSU243	Leyland Tiger TRCTL11/3R	Plaxton Paramount 3200	C57F	1983	
OJI3907	Leyland Tiger TRCTL11/3R	Plaxton Paramount 3200	C57F	1983	Ex B J Coaches, London SE2, 1988
GJI7173	Leyland Tiger TRCTL11/3R	Plaxton Paramount 3200	C53F	1983	Ex United, 1989
WXI6274	Mercedes-Benz L307D	Reeve Burgess	M12	1984	Ex Ramsey, Elsrickle, 1988
B177SFH	Leyland Tiger TRCTL11/3RH	Plaxton Paramount 3500 II	C46FT	1985	Ex Cheltenham & Gloucester, 1993
B178SFH	Leyland Tiger TRCTL11/3RH	Plaxton Paramount 3500 II	C49FT	1985	Ex Cheltenham & Gloucester, 1993
OKI9100	Leyland Royal Tiger RT	Plaxton Paramount 3500	C55F	1986	Ex Horseman, Reading, 1992

Previous Registrations:

AAU136A	FAU46L		CSU243	FJO603Y	OJI3907	YFG366Y
B177SFH	B215NDG, 511CHU	CSU432	MHR847X	OKI9100	C801FMC
B178SFH	B216NDG, HIL6075	GJI7173	AEF29Y	WXI6274	A841UGB

Livery: Two-tone blue

Charlton Services has predecessors in Charlton-on-Otmoor which go back to the 1920s. The local service from there, and just beyond, to Oxford has been established since that time. However, the vehicle seen here is on coaching duties. EDF269T, a Plaxton-bodied Leyland Leopard photographed in the gyratory traffic system in Parliament Square. *Keith Grimes*

CHENEY COACHES

Cheney Coaches Ltd, Cheney House, Thorpe Drive, Thorpe Industrial Estate,
Banbury, Oxfordshire, OX16 8UZ

URH13R	Bedford YMT	Plaxton Supreme III Express	C53F	1977	Acquired 1994
NFF945S	Bedford VAS5	Plaxton Supreme III Express	DP29F	1977	Acquired 1994
9785SM	Bedford YMT	Plaxton Supreme IV	C53F	1979	Ex Tappins, Didcot, 1994
PDN873	Bedford YMT(Cummins)	Plaxton Supreme IV	C53F	1979	Ex Tappins, Didcot, 1994
VPF742	Bedford YMT(Cummins)	Plaxton Supreme IV	C53F	1979	Ex Tappins, Didcot, 1994
OGL849	Bedford YMT	Plaxton Supreme IV	C53F	1979	Ex Tappins, Didcot, 1993
NSU914	Bedford YLQ	Plaxton Supreme IV Express	C45F	1980	Ex Dorset Police, 1994
URT682	Leyland Leopard PSU5/2L	Plaxton Paramount 3200	C53F	1982	Ex Goldstar Midlands, Chilwell, 1993
B586EGT	Renault-Dodge S56	Dormobile	B22FL	1985	Ex LB Merton, 1994
YSU975	TAZ D3200	TAZ Dubrava	C53F	1989	Ex Coaches, 1993
USU800	Iveco 315	Caetano Algarve	C28F	1990	

Previous Registrations:

9785SM	YAN817T	PDN873	YAN818T	VPF742	YAN819T
NSU914	KPR329W	URT682	?	YSU975	F794TBC
OGL849	YAN823T	USU800	DFE361X		

Livery: White blue and red

Cheney Coaches operate in the Banbury area using a varety of vehicles to meet its service requirements. Shrouded in mist on the bus station in the town is B269TLJ, a Mercedes-Benz L608D with a Reeve Burgess body conversion recently taken out of service. The ribbed side panels of the lieferwagen (van) are still visible on the window pillars. Interestingly, recent models have dropped the L from the badge and the 1994 catalogue shows them as kastenwagens (boxvans). *Keith Grimes*

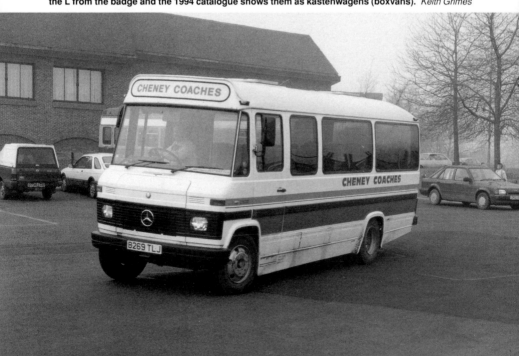

CHILTERN QUEENS

Chiltern Queens Ltd, Long Toll, Greenmore Hill, Woodcote,
Oxfordshire, RG8 0RP

TUD167G	AEC Reliance 6U3ZR	Plaxton Elite	C57F	1969	
FPX701H	AEC Reliance 6U3ZR	Plaxton Elite	C51F	1970	Ex Byng, Portsmouth, 1972
ABW777J	AEC Reliance 6U3ZR	Plaxton Elite II	C53F	1971	
EUD256K	AEC Reliance 6MU4R	Plaxton Derwent	B47F	1972	
OJO835M	Leyland Leopard PSU3B/4R	Plaxton Derwent	B55F	1974	
HCS795N	Leyland Leopard PSU3/3R	Alexander AYS	B53F	1975	Ex Clydeside Scottish, 1987
VBW581	Leyland Leopard PSU5A/4R	Plaxton Supreme III	C57F	1976	
RFC10T	Leyland Leopard PSU3E/4R	Duple Dominant II Express	C49F	1978	Ex Oxford Bus Company, 1989
RFC12T	Leyland Leopard PSU3E/4R	Duple Dominant II Express	C49F	1978	Ex Oxford Bus Company, 1990
WUD815T	Leyland Leopard PSU3E/4R	Duple Dominant II Express	C49F	1978	Ex Oxford Bus Company, 1990
591STT	Leyland Leopard PSU3E/4R	Plaxton Supreme IV Express	C53F	1979	
YFC18V	Leyland Leopard PSU3E/4R	Duple Dominant II Express	C49F	1979	Ex Oxford Bus Company, 1991
BBW22V	Leyland Leopard PSU3E/4R	Duple Dominant II Express	C49F	1979	Ex Oxford Bus Company, 1992
LUA244V	Volvo B58-61	Plaxton Supreme IV	C51F	1980	Ex Parry, Leominster, 1985
MUD25W	Leyland Leopard PSU3F/4R	Duple Dominant II Express	C49F	1981	Ex Oxford Bus Company, 1993
PPJ65W	Leyland Leopard PSU5C/4R	Wadham Stringer Vanguard	B54F	1982	Ex M o D, 1993
B911SPR	Volvo B10M-61	Plaxton Paramount 3200 II	C53F	1985	Ex Excelsior, Bournemouth, 1987
C644SJM	Volvo B10M-61	Plaxton Paramount 3200 II	C53F	1986	
C114PUJ	Volvo B10M-61	Caetano Algarve	C49FT	1986	Ex Hughes, Llanfair Caereinion, 1993
D262HFX	Volvo B10M-61	Plaxton Paramount 3200 III	C53F	1987	Ex Excelsior, Bournemouth, 1988
E533PRU	Volvo B10M-61	Plaxton Paramount 3200 III	C48FT	1987	
F344TSC	Mercedes-Benz 811D	Alexander AM	DP29F	1988	Ex Challenger, Bridgnorth, 1992
F986TTF	Mercedes-Benz 811D	Optare StarRider	B33F	1989	Ex Davron Travel, Caversham, 1991
H788RWJ	Scania K93CRB	Plaxton Paramount 3200 III	C55F	1990	

Previous Registrations:

591STT	UUD623T	C114PUJ	C690KDS, SEL7X	VBW581	SFC32P
BMO891T	48AC88	PPJ65W	50AC08		

Livery: Red and white; Two-tone green and white (coaches)

Wearing a livery of poppy red and white is Chiltern Queens' YFC18V, a Leyland Leopard with Duple Dominant II Express bodywork. Ordered by National Bus company and allocated to City of Oxford, now known as the Oxford Bus Company, the vehicle is seen near its original home, working the local service between Peppard and Reading. *Colin Lloyd*

For very many years Chiltern Queens was renowned as an operator of AEC Reliances, many of which were purchased new. A few of these remain. More recently the choice for the coaching fleet has been Plaxton-bodied Volvo B10Ms. C644SJM was a new vehicle when it joined the fleet in May 1986. The vehicle was at Epsom for the Derby when photographed. *Ivor Norman*

Two Mercedes-Benz 811D midibuses are operated by Chiltern Queens and they feature contrasting coachwork. F334TSC carries Alexander bodywork with high-back seating while F986TTF has bus seats and DiPTAC features in the stylish Optare StarRider body. *Colin Lloyd*

CITY BUSLINES

City Buslines Ltd, 386 Park Road, Hockley, Birmingham
West Midlands, B18 5ST

TPD192M	Leyland National 1051/1R	B40D	1974	Ex Busylink, Hemel Hempstead, 1993
WPG219M	Leyland National 10351/1R	B44F	1974	Ex Horsham Coaches, 1993
GUG113N	Leyland National 11351/1R	B52F	1974	Ex Warren, Ticehurst, 1993
GOL400N	Leyland National 11351/1R	B49F	1975	Ex Northumbria, 1993
GLJ682N	Leyland National 11351/1R/SC	DP48F	1975	Ex Wilts & Dorset, 1993
LJN663P	Leyland National 11351/1R	B52F	1975	Ex Sovereign Bus & Coach, 1993
RHB306R	Leyland National 10351A/1R	B41F	1977	Ex Hallamshire Bus Co, 1993
NWO465R	Leyland National 11351A/1R	DP48F	1977	Ex Burrows, Ogmore Vale, 1993
RBU178R	Leyland National 11351A/1R	B49F	1977	Ex G M Buses, 1993
NEN954R	Leyland National 11351A/1R	B49F	1977	Ex Thanet Bus, Ramsgate, 1993
YPF775T	Leyland National 10351A/1R	B41F	1979	Ex Sovereign Bus & Coach, 1993
DPH499T	Leyland National 10351B/1R	B41F	1979	Ex Sovereign Bus & Coach, 1993
DDW431V	Leyland National 10351A/1R	B41F	1980	Ex Hallamshire Bus Co, 1993

Livery: Green and white

One of the newest operators to start local stage services in Birmingham, in competition with West Midlands Travel, is City Buslines which was formed in November 1993. All the units are Leyland Nationals which came from many parts of the country. GUG113N, from Yorkshire via Kent, is seen awaiting departure at the terminus in Quinton Road West, Birmingham. *Tim Weatherup*

CLARIBELS

Claribel Coaches Ltd, 10 Fortnum Close, Tile Cross, Birmingham
West Midlands, B33 0LG

JOX458P	Leyland Leopard PSU3C/4R	Plaxton Supreme III Express	C49F	1976	Ex Midland Red West, 1993
MAW112P	Ford R1114	Plaxton Supreme III	C49F	1976	Ex Allenways, Birmingham, 1991
PHH613R	Leyland Leopard PSU3E/4R	Duple Dominant	C49F	1978	Ex Midland Fox, 1993
BGY589T	Leyland Leopard PSU5C/4R	Plaxton Supreme IV	C48FT	1979	Ex Yardleys, Birmingham, 1993
JMB330T	Leyland Leopard PSU3E/4R	Duple Dominant II Express	C53F	1979	Ex Stephenson, Rochford, 1993
JMB337T	Leyland Leopard PSU3E/4R	Duple Dominant II Express	C53F	1979	Ex Stephenson, Rochford, 1993
ODM501V	Leyland Leopard PSU3E/4R	Duple Dominant II Express	C53F	1979	Ex Stephenson, Rochford, 1993
KRO645V	Ford R1114	Duple Dominant II	C53F	1980	Ex Golden Boy, Hoddesdon, 1986
WCK132V	Leyland Leopard PSU3E/4R	Duple Dominant II Express	C49F	1980	Ex Midland Red North, 1993
FYX812W	Leyland Leopard PSU3E/4R	Duple Dominant II Express	C49F	1980	Ex Phil Anslow, Garndiffaith, 1994
FYX823W	Leyland Leopard PSU3E/4R	Duple Dominant II Express	C49F	1980	Ex Phil Anslow, Garndiffaith, 1994
WWA299Y	Leyland Tiger TRCTL11/3R	Plaxton Paramount 3500	C51F	1983	Ex Allenways, Birmingham, 1992
YGY638Y	Leyland Tiger TRCTL11/3R	Plaxton Paramount 3500	C50F	1983	Ex Allenways, Birmingham, 1992
D900MWR	Freight Rover Sherpa	Dormobile	B20F	1987	Ex Yorkshire Rider, 1991
E53TYG	Leyland Royal Tiger RTC	Leyland Doyen	C53FT	1988	Ex Allenways, Birmingham, 1993
F32KHS	Hestair-Duple 425 SDA1512	Duple 425	C53FT	1989	Ex Allenways, Birmingham, 1993
F472RPG	Renault Trafic	Jubilee	M11	1989	Ex van, 1990
G368MFD	Ford Transit VE6	Ford	M12	1990	Acquired 1992
G155XJF	Toyota Coaster HB31R	Caetano Optimo	C21F	1990	Ex Allenways, Birmingham, 1992

Livery: White and blue

Long established as a coach operator, Claribels of Birmingham has recently started the commercial operation of local services. Route 94 is the main route from Birmingham City Centre to Chelmsley Wood. A Leyland Leopard with Duple Dominant II Express bodywork, JMB337T, is at the Bull Street terminus in the City. This vehicle originated with Crosville passing to Crosville Wales in 1986 and is one of a trio of similar vehicles that have remained together ever since. *Tim Weatherup*

CRESSWELL

N N Cresswell, Coach House, Worcester Road, Evesham,
Hereford & Worcester, WR11 4RA

HVN601N	Bedford YRQ	Plaxton Elite III	C45F	1975	Ex Owen's Motors, Knighton, 1984
PJI8917	Bedford YMT	Plaxton Supreme III	C53F	1978	Ex Westours, Pershore, 1993
SDR450T	Volvo B58-61	Duple Dominant II	C57F	1979	Ex Brimm, Honeybourne, 1992
XCJ750T	Bedford YMT	Plaxton Supreme IV Express	C53F	1979	
KPT583T	Bedford YMT	Plaxton Supreme IV	C53F	1979	Ex Norrie, New Deer, 1988
AUJ715T	Bedford YMT	Duple Dominant II	C53F	1979	Ex Go-Whittle, Highley, 1982
FUJ938V	Bedford YMT	Duple Dominant II	C53F	1980	Ex Owen, Oswestry, 1988
FUJ950V	Bedford YMT	Plaxton Supreme IV	C53F	1980	Ex Go-Whittle, Highley, 1983
JRB663V	Bedford YMT	Plaxton Supreme IV	C53F	1980	Ex Kime, Folkingham, 1993
RPU526W	Bedford CF	Reeve Burgess	C17F	1980	Ex College, Malvern, 1991
LIB1797	Bedford YNT	Plaxton Supreme IV	C53F	1981	Ex Hilo, Sandy, 1991
LCJ626Y	Bedford YNT	Plaxton Paramount 3200 E	C53F	1983	
B180TVJ	Bedford YNT	Plaxton Paramount 3200 II	C53F	1985	
C175HYD	Bedford YNV Venturer	Duple Laser 2	C57F	1986	Ex Coleman, Yeovil, 1988
C48HKK	Bedford YNV Venturer	Plaxton Paramount 3200 II	C53F	1986	Ex Camden, Sevenoaks, 1993
D827PUK	Freight Rover Sherpa	Carlyle	B18F	1987	Ex Ribble, 1992
J2NNC	MAN 10-180	Caetano Algarve II	C35F	1991	

Previous Registrations:

LIB1797	KKW451W	PJI8917	URX524S, RJB895

Livery: White and red

Evesham-based operator Cresswell operate this Bedford CF minibus on local services. The bodywork is that from Reeve Burgess, to a style known then as Reebur, and typical of the style of the late 1970s and early 1980s. It is seen in April 1994. *Bill Potter*

DAVID R GRASBY

D R Grasby, Windmill Farm, Banbury Road, Oxhill, Warwickshire, CV35 0RP

KUC968P	Leyland Fleetline FE30AGR	MCW	H44/29F	1976	Ex Best of British, Stratford, 1985
YPL92T	AEC Reliance 6U2R	Duple Dominant II Express	C53F	1979	Ex London Country, 1986
YPL102T	AEC Reliance 6U2R	Duple Dominant II Express	C53F	1979	Ex London Country, 1985
YPL105T	AEC Reliance 6U2R	Duple Dominant II Express	C53F	1979	Ex London Country, 1985
EPM134V	AEC Reliance 6U2R	Duple Dominant II Express	C53F	1980	Ex London Country, 1986
MKV86V	Ford R1114	Plaxton Supreme IV Express	C53F	1980	
MKV87V	Ford R1014	Plaxton Supreme IV	C45F	1980	
3669DG	Volvo B10M-61	Plaxton Supreme V	C53F	1982	
ANA435Y	DAF MB200DKTL600	Plaxton Paramount 3200	C53F	1983	Ex Shearings, 1989
B21AUS	DAF MB200DKFL600	Van Hool Alizée	C48FT	1985	Ex Haldane, Glasgow, 1987
C328DND	Volvo B10M-61	Van Hool Alizée	C53F	1986	Ex Shearings, 1991
6267AC	Volvo B10M-61	Ikarus Blue Danube	C53F	1987	

Previous Registrations:

3669DG	YKV811X	6267AC	E422KAC

Livery: Yellow and black

David Grasby of Oxhill is one of the few operators to have a yellow and black livery for its vehicles.
YPL102T is seen here in Leamington. This vehicle is one of four former London Country, Duple
Dominant-bodied AEC Reliances in the fleet. *Phillip Stephenson*

DE LUXE

De Luxe Coach Services Ltd, 49 Long Street, Atherstone, Warwickshire, CV9 1AZ

Depots: Mancetter Road, Atherstone.

RPT293K	Leyland Leopard PSU3B/4R	Alexander AY	DP47F	1972	Ex Reed, Sunnyside, 1992
DRB61T	Leyland Leopard PSU5C/4R	Plaxton Supreme IV	C57F	1979	Ex Dons, Dunmow, 1992
EWW208T	Leyland Leopard PSU3E/4R	Plaxton Supreme IV	C46F	1979	Ex Spencer, New Ollerton, 1984
LDS381V	Leyland Leopard PSU3E/4R	Plaxton Supreme IV	C53F	1980	Ex Garelochhead CS, 1981
LBO10X	Volvo B10M-61	Plaxton Viewmaster IV	C53F	1981	Ex Bebb, Llantwit Fardre, 1985
LBO11X	Volvo B10M-61	Plaxton Viewmaster IV	C51F	1981	Ex Bebb, Llantwit Fardre, 1984
YEH182X	Volvo B10M-61	Duple Dominant IV	C53F	1981	Ex Baker, Biddulph, 1985
YFJ68X	Volvo B10M-61	Duple Dominant IV	C53F	1982	Ex SUT, Sheffield, 1987
XVC230X	Leyland Leopard PSU5C/4R	Plaxton Supreme IV	C57F	1982	

Previous Registrations:

YEH182X	FHS738X, 3471RU	YFJ68X	OHE269X, 951RMX

Livery: Red, white and black

De-Luxe have a pair of Plaxton Viewmaster-bodied Volvos new to the south Wales operator, Bebb of Llantwit Fardre. LBO11X, seen here displaying the deep windscreen feature of this design, was purchased in 1984, the sister vehicle being added the following year when found to be for sale at a dealers. *Bill Potter*

DRM

D R Morris, Coach Garage, Broadbridge, Hereford & Worcester, HR7 4NT

Depot: Stourport Road, Bromyard.

MOI3512	Volvo B58-61	Plaxton Elite III Express	C53F	1972	Ex Down, Mary Tavy, 1986
MOI5633	AEC Reliance 6U3ZR	Plaxton Elite III Express	C49F	1972	
MOI1793	Leyland Leopard PSU3E/4R	Plaxton Supreme III Express	C53F	1977	
RKA871T	Leyland National 11351A/1R(Volvo)		B49F	1978	Ex Alpine, Llandudno, 1993
MOI3565	Volvo B10M-56	Plaxton Supreme VI Express	C50F	1982	Ex Harding's, Redditch, 1992
MOI9565	Volvo B10M-61	Jonckheere Jubilee P50	C53FT	1983	Ex Budden's, Woodfalls, 1988
MOI7000	Volvo B10M-61	Jonckheere Jubilee P50	C49FT	1988	Ex Coliseum, West End, 1993

Previous Registrations:

MOI1793	OVJ400R	MOI3565	KWP111X	MOI7000	SLU195, E562LDL
MOI3512	KEG773L, 5635CD	MOI5633	OKX49L	MOI9565	NNV554Y

Livery: White and grey

With a dateless registration and a Plaxton Supreme IV front succesfully hiding its 21 years of age, DRM Volvo MOI3512 is seen leaving Hereford on its regular route to Ledbury. *Martin Perry*

DUDLEY'S

Dudley Coaches Ltd, Poplar Garage, Radford, Inkberrow,
Hereford & Worcester, WR7 4LS

UWP96R	Ford R1114	Plaxton Supreme III Express	C53F	1976	
TWP97V	Ford R1114	Plaxton Supreme IV Express	C53F	1980	
GVP952W	Ford R1114	Plaxton Supreme IV	C53F	1980	Ex Royal, Redditch, 1985
JWB847W	Leyland Leopard PSU5D/5R	Plaxton Supreme IV	C57F	1980	Ex Royal, Redditch, 1986
MIW1607	Volvo B58-61	Van Hool Alizée	C52F	1980	Ex Warner, Tewkesbury, 1987
UOI7274	Volvo B58-56	Plaxton Supreme IV Express	C48FT	1980	Ex DRM, Bromyard, 1988
KHL460W	Volvo B58-56	Plaxton Supreme IV	C53F	1981	Ex Woodstones, Kidderminster, 1988
CIL9223	Leyland Leopard PSU5C/4R	Plaxton Supreme IV	C57F	1981	Ex Royal, Redditch, 1986
STO244X	Leyland Leopard PSU3F/5R	Plaxton Supreme IV	C53F	1981	Ex Royal, Redditch, 1986
KUY98X	Ford R1114	Plaxton Supreme V Express	C53F	1982	
A722BAB	Volvo B10M-61	Duple Caribbean	C51FT	1984	
B951TKV	Leyland Tiger TRCTL11/3RZ	Plaxton Paramount 3500 II	C53F	1985	Ex Richardson, Midhurst, 1994
FIL7615	DAF SB2300DHTD585	Plaxton Paramount 3200	C57F	1984	Ex Gilchrist, East Kilbride, 1991
C319UFP	Volvo B10M-61	Plaxton Paramount 3200 II	C57F	1986	Ex Crawford, Neilston, 1989
C685MWJ	Volvo B10M-61	Plaxton Paramount 3200 III	C57F	1986	Ex Bere Regis & District, 1994
D225LWY	Volvo B10M-61	Plaxton Paramount 3500 III	C53F	1987	Ex Wallace Arnold, 1993

Previous Registrations:

B951TKV	684DYX	MIW1607	SFH655W
C685MWJ	OJT568	SFH655W	BSF337W, 9246WF
CIL9223	BGS288X	UOI7274	ECJ700W
FIL7615	7391MH, A334FRB		

Livery: Cream and two-tone green

The garage and operating centre of Dudley's Coaches is deep in rural Worcestershire (the legendary location of Ambridge), but their sphere of operations is very wide. JWB847W was photographed in Weston-super-Mare and is a Plaxton-bodied Leyland Leopard which was acquired with the business of Royal Motorways of Redditch in 1986. *Richard Eversden*

FALCON

AS Sahota & SS Sarai, Sahota Centre, Heath Street, Smethwick,
West Midlands, B66 2QZ

WNO558L	Leyland National 1151/1R/0401	B52F	1973	Ex East Midland, 1994
XRR584M	Leyland National 1151/2R/0403	B44F	1973	Ex East Midland, 1994
SGR565R	Leyland National 11351A/1R	B49F	1976	Ex Waddell, Lochwinnoch, 1993
NEN958R	Leyland National 11351A/1R	B49F	1977	Ex Thanet Bus, Ramsgate, 1993
VFX983S	Leyland National 11351A/1R	B49F	1978	Ex Wilts & Dorset, 1993
XNG773S	Leyland National 11351A/1R	B52F	1978	Ex Thanet Bus, Ramsgate, 1993
WBN478T	Leyland National 11351A/1R	B49F	1979	Ex Thanet Bus, Ramsgate, 1993

Livery: Maroon and Cream

Falcon Travel is a newcomer to local bus services. Although based in Smethwick, the main service operated is trunk route 50 from Birmingham City Centre to the Maypole in competition with West Midlands Travel and Your Bus. Leyland National NEN958R, while new to Lancashire United, came from Thanet Bus of Ramsgate in October 1993 and is seen on service 15, in Digbeth. *Keith Grimes*

FLIGHTS

Flights Coach Travel Ltd, 294/6 Soho Road, Handsworth,
Birmingham, West Midlands, B21 9LY

F700COA	Volvo B10M-53	Plaxton Paramount 4000 III	CH55/12DT	1989	
F701COA	Volvo B10M-53	Plaxton Paramount 4000 III	CH55/12DT	1989	
F702COA	Volvo B10M-53	Plaxton Paramount 4000 III	CH55/12DT	1989	
F703COA	Volvo B10M-53	Plaxton Paramount 4000 III	CH55/12DT	1989	
F704COA	Volvo B10M-53	Plaxton Paramount 4000 III	CH55/12DT	1989	
F707COA	Volvo B10M-53	Plaxton Paramount 4000 III	CH55/12DT	1989	
F708COA	Volvo B10M-53	Plaxton Paramount 4000 III	CH55/12DT	1989	
F709COA	Volvo B10M-53	Plaxton Paramount 4000 III	CH55/12DT	1989	
F710COA	Volvo B10M-53	Plaxton Paramount 4000 III	CH55/12DT	1989	
1FTO	Bova FHD12.280	Bova Futura	C25FT	1989	Ex Central Coachways, 1993
G717JOG	Volvo B10M-53	Plaxton Paramount 4000 III	CH55/12DT	1990	
G720JOG	Volvo B10M-53	Plaxton Paramount 4000 III	CH55/12DT	1990	
G727JOG	Volvo B10M-53	Plaxton Paramount 4000 III	CH55/12DT	1990	
H2FTG	Toyota Coaster HDB30R	Caetano Optimo II	C18F	1991	
H3FTG	Toyota Coaster HDB30R	Caetano Optimo II	C18F	1991	
J4FTG	Toyota Coaster HDB30R	Caetano Optimo II	C21F	1992	
J6FTG	Toyota Coaster HDB30R	Caetano Optimo II	C21F	1992	
J7FTG	Mercedes-Benz 811D	PMT Ami	C33F	1992	
J8FTG	Mercedes-Benz 811D	PMT Ami	C33F	1992	
J10FTG	Mercedes-Benz 811D	PMT Ami	C33F	1992	
K12FTG	Volvo B10M-60	Plaxton Excalibur	C49FT	1992	
K14FTG	Volvo B10M-60	Plaxton Excalibur	C49FT	1993	
K15FTG	Volvo B10M-60	Plaxton Excalibur	C49FT	1993	
K16FTG	Volvo B10M-60	Plaxton Excalibur	C49FT	1993	
K17FTG	Volvo B10M-60	Plaxton Excalibur	C49FT	1993	
K18FTG	Volvo B10M-60	Plaxton Excalibur	C49FT	1993	
K19FTG	Volvo B10M-60	Plaxton Excalibur	C49FT	1993	
K20FTG	Volvo B10M-60	Plaxton Excalibur	C49FT	1993	
L FTG	Bova FHD12.290	Bova Futura	C44FT	1994	
L FTG	Bova FHD12.290	Bova Futura	C44FT	1994	
L FTG	Bova FHD12.290	Bova Futura	C44FT	1994	
L FTG	Bova FHD12.290	Bova Futura	C44FT	1994	
L FTG	Bova FHD12.290	Bova Futura	C44FT	1994	
L FTG	Bova FHD12.290	Bova Futura	C44FT	1994	
L FTG	Bova FHD12.290	Bova Futura	C44FT	1994	
L FTG	Bova FHD12.290	Bova Futura	C44FT	1994	

Previous Registrations:
1FTO   F907CJW, 245DOC

Livery: Cream, black and silver.

Opposite, above: **Flights of Birmingham has four Toyota/Caetano Optimo small coaches. Two of these seat 18, while the other pair seat 21. J4FTG shown here is one of the latter. They are often used as feeders from Wolverhampton to the main airport coach service at Birmingham though, as seen here, J4FTG has operated through to Heathrow.** *Colin Lloyd*

Opposite, bottom: **A fleet of twelve tri-axle Volvo B10M-53s is owned by Flights to maintain their frequent Manchester-Birmingham-Coventry-Heathrow-Gatwick Airport service and these are also available for private hire. They feature Plaxton Paramount 4000 bodywork with 55 seats upstairs and 12 in the rear saloon, a necessary feature of such bodies on this mid-engined chassis. F710COA was photographed on a private charter in Brighton.** *Keith Grimes*

G & G Travel was formerly a member of the Western Travel Group. That group was purchased in December 1993 by Stagecoach and this operator shares a depot in Leamington with sister company Midland Red South. Some of the coaches in the fleet are regularly employed on local service work. 1089, B72OKV (though recently re-registered A7GGT) is a Leyland Tiger with Plaxton Paramount 3200 bodywork which was transferred in from the Midland Red South fleet. *Ken Crawley*

1086, CSV219, is the only double deck coach in the G & G fleet and is a MCW Metroliner, new in 1985. It had brought the Rugby Male Voice Choir to Cardiff when photographed. *Richard Eversden*

G & G

G & G Travel Ltd, Station Approach, Leamington Spa, Warwickshire, CV31 3SA

(A member of Stagecoach Holdings plc)

29	NAK29X	Leyland Leopard PSU3F/4R	Duple Dominant IV	C47F	1981	Ex East Midland, 1994
30	NAK30X	Leyland Leopard PSU3F/4R	Duple Dominant IV	C47F	1981	Ex East Midland, 1994

1019	A848VML	Leyland Leopard PSU3E/4R	Duple Dominant IV (1983)	C53F	1979	Ex Grey-Green, London N16, 1987
1020	9984PG	Leyland Leopard PSU3E/4R	Duple Dominant II Express	C53F	1980	Ex Grey-Green, London N16, 1988
1021	MUV837X	Leyland Leopard PSU5C/4R	Duple Dominant IV	C53F	1982	Ex Grey-Green, London N16, 1988
1059	E630KCX	DAF SB2305DHTD585	Duple 320	C55F	1988	Ex Gray, Hoyland Common, 1990
1058	C253HJX	DAF MB200DKFL600	Duple Caribbean 2	C53F	1985	Ex Hughes-DAF, 1993
1068	WSU293	Volvo B10M-60	Plaxton Paramount 3200 III	C49F	1990	Ex Cheltenham & Gloucester, 1993
1086	CSV219	MCW Metroliner DR130/6	MCW	CH55/19FT	1984	Ex Go-Ahead Northern, 1992
1087	498FYB	Leyland Tiger TRCTL11/3R	Plaxton Paramount 3200	C50F	1983	Ex Cheltenham & Gloucester, 1993
1088	A8GGT	Leyland Tiger TRCTL11/3R	Plaxton Paramount 3200 E	C57F	1983	Ex Cheltenham & Gloucester, 1993
1089	A7GGT	Leyland Tiger TRCTL11/3RH	Plaxton Paramount 3200	C51F	1985	Ex Midland Red South, 1992
1458	D458CKV	Freight Rover Sherpa 365	Rootes	B16F	1986	Ex Midland Red South, 1992
1464	D464CKV	Freight Rover Sherpa 365	Rootes	B16F	1986	Ex Midland Red South, 1992
1475	D475CKV	Freight Rover Sherpa 365	Rootes	B16F	1986	Ex Midland Red South, 1990
1477	E77PUH	Freight Rover Sherpa 405	Carlyle Citybus 2	B20F	1987	Ex Red & White, 1991
1490	E95OUH	Freight Rover Sherpa 405	Carlyle Citybus 2	B20F	1987	Ex Red & White, 1991
1491	E99OUH	Freight Rover Sherpa 405	Carlyle Citybus 2	B20F	1987	Ex Red & White, 1991
1820	F660PWK	Leyland Lynx LX112L10ZR1R	Leyland Lynx	B51F	1988	
1821	F661PWK	Leyland Lynx LX112L10ZR1R	Leyland Lynx	B51F	1988	
1930	LHT724P	Bristol VRT/SL3/501(6LXB)	Eastern Coach Works	H39/31F	1976	Ex Swindon & District, 1992
1931	MAU145P	Bristol VRT/SL3/6LXB	Eastern Coach Works	H43/31F	1976	Ex Bluebird, 1993
1932	ONH846P	Bristol VRT/SL3/6LXB	Eastern Coach Works	H43/31F	1976	Ex Bluebird, 1993
1933	PEU516R	Bristol VRT/SL3/6LXB	Eastern Coach Works	H43/31F	1977	Ex Swindon & District, 1992
1950	WWM930W	Leyland Atlantean AN68B/1R	Willowbrook	H45/33F	1981	Ex Merseybus, 1989
1951	WWM936W	Leyland Atlantean AN68B/1R	Willowbrook	H45/33F	1981	Ex Merseybus, 1989
1952	AFY192X	Leyland Atlantean AN68B/1R	Willowbrook	H45/33F	1982	Ex Merseybus, 1989
1956	SDA651S	Leyland Fleetline FE30AGR	Park Royal	H43/33F	1978	Ex West Midlands Travel, 1990
1957	SDA715S	Leyland Fleetline FE30AGR	MCW	H43/33F	1978	Ex West Midlands Travel, 1990
1958	WDA994T	Leyland Fleetline FE30AGR	MCW	H43/33F	1979	Ex West Midlands Travel, 1990

Previous Registrations:

498FYB	CDG207Y	A848VML	FRA64V	CSV219	B231XEU
9984PG	FYX815W	A8GGT	A202RHT	WSU293	From new
A7GGT	B72OKV				

Livery: Stagecoach white, orange, red and blue replacing two-tone blue and white

GLENSTUART

Glenstuart Travel Ltd, Premier House, Darlington Street, Wolverhampton,
West Midlands, WV1 4NS

GCY751N	Leyland National 11351/1R		B52F	1974	Ex Zamir, Burton, 1993
AEF765A	Leyland Leopard PSU3C/4R	Plaxton Supreme III	C49F	1976	Ex Ash, Woburn Moor, 1993
WRN13R	Leyland Leopard PSU4D/4R	Alexander AY	DP45F	1977	Ex Ogden's, Haydock, 1992
WRN14R	Leyland Leopard PSU4D/4R	Alexander AY	DP45F	1977	Ex Ogden's, Haydock, 1992
RJF403R	Bedford YLQ	Willowbrook 001	B47F	1977	Ex Phillips Coachways, 1993
TTV754X	Renault-Dodge S56	Reeve Burgess	B27F	1982	Ex Jeavons, Tipton, 1992
B143ACK	Leyland Tiger TRCTL11/3R	Duple Caribbean	C48F	1985	Ex Ellison, Ashton Keynes, 1992

Previous Registrations:
AEF765A   JOX460P

Livery: White, maroon and yellow

**TTV754X, in the corporate white, maroon and yellowed-livery, is the only small vehicle in the
Glenstuart fleet. It is a Reeve Burgess-bodied Renault-Dodge S56 originally in the Nottinghamshire
County Council fleet, and latterly with Jeavons of Tipton. Glenstuart operate route 507 from
Wolverhampton to Pendeford.** *Phillip Stephenson*

GO WHITTLE

R A & D L Whittle, Corvedale Motor Co Ltd, & M & M Coaches Ltd,
105 Coventry St, Kidderminster, Hereford & Worcester, DY10 2BH

Depots: Central Garage, Alveley; Lion Lane, Cleobury Mortimer; High Street, Highley; Mouse Lane, Kidderminster and Fishmore Road, Ludlow.

1	ODN601	Leyland Leopard PSU5D/4R	Duple Dominant III	C57F	1980	
2	G102JNP	Dennis Javelin 12SDA1931	Plaxton Paramount 3200 III	C51F	1990	
3	F903RWP	Dennis Javelin 12SDA1917	Plaxton Paramount 3200 III	C57F	1989	
4	F904RWP	Dennis Javelin 12SDA1917	Plaxton Paramount 3200 III	C57F	1989	
5	JPY505	Bedford YNT	Duple Dominant IV	C53F	1982	
6	K6GOW	Dennis Dart 9.8SDL3017	Northern Counties Paladin	B42F	1992	
7	F907RWP	Dennis Javelin 12SDA1917	Plaxton Paramount 3200 III	C53F	1989	
8	G108JNP	Dennis Javelin 12SDA1931	Plaxton Paramount 3200 III	C51F	1990	
10	RCE510	Freight Rover Sherpa	Carlyle	B18F	1987	Ex Bee Line Buzz, 1991
11	G111JNP	Dennis Javelin 12SDA1931	Plaxton Paramount 3200 III	C51F	1990	
12	SIJ4712	Dennis Javelin 12SDA1917	Plaxton Paramount 3200 III	C57F	1989	
14	RPP514	Bedford YMT	Plaxton Supreme IV	C53F	1980	Ex Narburgh, Alveley, 1990
15	F115TWP	Mercedes-Benz 811D	Reeve Burgess Beaver	C33F	1989	
16	F116TWP	Freight Rover Sherpa	Crystals	C16F	1989	
17	H17GOW	Dennis Javelin 12SDA1929	Plaxton Paramount 3200 III	C53F	1991	
18	FUJ918V	Bedford YMT	Duple Dominant II	C53F	1980	
19	H19GOW	Dennis Javelin 12SDA1929	Plaxton Paramount 3200 III	C53F	1991	
21	K21OUY	Volvo B10M-60	Plaxton Premiére 350	C53F	1993	
24	FUJ924V	Bedford YMT	Duple Dominant II	C57F	1980	
29	G29HDW	Dennis Javelin 12SDA1907	Duple 320	C57F	1990	Ex Bebb, Llantwitt Fardre, 1992
30	G130JNP	Dennis Javelin 12SDA1930	Plaxton Paramount 3200 III	C51F	1990	
30A	G30HDW	Dennis Javelin 12SDA1907	Duple 320	C57F	1990	Ex Bebb, Llantwitt Fardre, 1992
31	G131JNP	Dennis Javelin 12SDA1931	Plaxton Paramount 3200 III	C51F	1990	
33	K33GOW	Dennis Dart 9.8SDL3017	Northern Counties Paladin	B42F	1992	

Dennis Javelins have been chosen by Go Whittle for their coach fleet in recent years. This Plaxton-bodied vehicle has a low driving position and Telma retarder fitted. No.2, G102JNP, is seen, unloading race-goers at Epsom.
Ivor Norman

35	LJJ35P	Bedford YLQ	Plaxton Supreme III	C45F	1976	Ex Narburgh, Alveley, 1990
36	K36OUY	Volvo B10M-60	Plaxton Premiére 350	C53F	1993	
37	K37OUY	Volvo B10M-60	Plaxton Premiére 350	C53F	1993	
39	F139TWP	Dennis Javelin 12SDA1917	Plaxton Paramount 3200 III	C53F	1989	
40	FUJ940V	Bedford YMT	Duple Dominant II	DP57F	1980	Ex M & M, Kidderminster, 1981
41	URH341	Leyland Leopard PSU5D/4R	Duple Dominant III	C57F	1980	
42	WTL642	Freight Rover Sherpa	Carlyle	B18F	1987	Ex Bee Line Buzz, 1991
43	YBA543Y	Ford Transit 160	Made-to-Measure	M12	1982	Ex Narburgh, Alveley, 1990
44	F244SAB	Dennis Javelin 12SDA1917	Plaxton Paramount 3200 III	C57F	1989	
46	YFU846	Bedford YLQ	Duple Dominant II	C45F	1978	Ex M & M, Kidderminster, 1981
46A	G46HDW	Dennis Javelin 12SDA1907	Duple 320	C57F	1990	Ex Bebb, Llantwitt Fardre, 1992
47	G47HDW	Dennis Javelin 12SDA1907	Duple 320	C57F	1990	Ex Bebb, Llantwitt Fardre, 1992
48	LSV548	Bedford YMT	Duple Dominant II	C53F	1978	Ex Narburgh, Alveley, 1990
48A	FUJ948V	Bedford YMT	Duple Dominant II	DP57F	1980	Ex M & M, Kidderminster, 1981
49	G49HDW	Dennis Javelin 12SDA1907	Duple 320	C57F	1990	Ex Bebb, Llantwit Fardre, 1992
51	F151TWP	Mercedes-Benz 811D	Reeve Burgess Beaver	C33F	1989	
51A	G51HDW	Dennis Javelin 12SDA1907	Duple 320	C57F	1990	Ex Bebb, Llantwit Fardre, 1992
52	F152TWP	Freight Rover Sherpa	Carlyle Citybus 2	C16F	1989	
52A	WVU152S	Bedford YMT	Duple Dominant II	C53F	1978	Ex Narburgh, Alveley, 1990
54	GBB254	Bedford YLQ	Duple Dominant II	C45F	1978	Ex M & M, Kidderminster, 1981
55	XKH455	Bedford YNT	Plaxton Supreme VI Express	C49F	1982	
87	TPJ287S	Bedford YMT	Duple Dominant II	C53F	1978	Ex Narburgh, Alveley, 1990

Previous Registrations:

A468MRW	A837PPP, 9258VC	RPP514	JPC783V, 6253VC, MWK826V
GBB254	VNT23S	SIJ4712	F112TWP
JPY505	ARB531T	URH341	KUX222W
LSV548	YHB647T	WTL642	D255OOJ .
ODN601	KUX221W	XKH455	PNT849X, GBB254, MAB117X
RCE510	D250OOJ	YFU846	VNT43S

Livery: White, blue, green and yellow

Go Whittle have two Dennis Darts, both supplied with Northern Counties bodywork in 1992 for tendered operations requiring vehicle with DiPTAC features. These received registrations to match their allocated fleet numbers which, as in most cases are the same as the last two digits of the index marks, are no longer displayed on the vehicle exteriors. No.6, K6GOW is seen here in Kidderminster from where is usually works the Bridgenorth service, while sister vehicle 33 is currently based in Ludlow. *Bill Potter*

GUIDE FRIDAY

Guide Friday Ltd, Civic Hall, 14 Rother Street, Stratford-upon-Avon,
Warwickshire, CV37 6LU

HKL826	AEC Regal 0662	Beadle	OB35F	1946	Ex Hastings & District, 1989
HKL836	AEC Regal 0662	Beadle	OB35F	1946	Ex Hastings & District, 1989
KNN622	Daimler CVD6	Massey	H22/28RD	1949	Ex Craswell, West Bromwich, 1993
CHL772	Daimler CVD6	Willowbrook	C35F	1950	Ex Hastings & District, 1989
264ERY	Leyland Titan PD3A/1	Park Royal	O41/33R	1963	Ex Leicester, 1978
XKO54A	Leyland Atlantean PDR1/1	Weymann	O44/33F	1963	Ex Robson, Thornaby, 1992
WJY759	Leyland Atlantean PDR1/1	Metro Cammell	O44/33F	1963	Ex Plymouth, 1991
CRU184C	Daimler Fleetline CRG6LX	Weymann	O45/29F	1965	Ex London Transport, 1984
GYS896D	Leyland Atlantean PDR1/1	Alexander A	O44/33F	1966	Ex Windsorian, Windsor, 1990
ERV250D	Leyland Atlantean PDR1/1	Metro Cammell	O44/33F	1966	Ex Southdown, 1991
ERV254D	Leyland Atlantean PDR1/1	Metro Cammell	O44/33F	1966	Ex Southdown, 1991
DWU839H	Bristol VRT/SL6G	Eastern Coach Works	O39/31F	1969	Ex York City & District, 1990
FWT956J	Bristol VRT/SL6G	Eastern Coach Works	O39/31F	1970	Ex York City & District, 1990
KHC813K	Leyland Atlantean PDR1A/1	East Lancashire	O45/31F	1972	Ex Eastbourne, 1988
KHC814K	Leyland Atlantean PDR1A/1	East Lancashire	O45/31F	1972	Ex Eastbourne, 1989
KHC815K	Leyland Atlantean PDR1A/1	East Lancashire	O45/31F	1972	Ex Eastbourne, 1989
KHC817K	Leyland Atlantean PDR1A/1	East Lancashire	O45/31F	1972	Ex Eastbourne, 1988
GHL191L	Bristol VRT/SL3/6LXB	Eastern Coach Works	O43/31F	1972	Ex Cambus, 1993
ETO161L	Daimler Fleetline CRG6LX	Willowbrook	O47/32F	1973	Ex Nottingham, 1985
ETO178L	Daimler Fleetline CRG6LX	Willowbrook	O47/32F	1973	Ex Nottingham, 1985
MLH304L	Daimler Fleetline CRG6LXB	MCW	O44/27F	1973	Ex Windsorian, Windsor, 1990
OTO542M	Leyland Atlantean AN68/1R	East Lancashire	O47/30D	1974	Ex Nottingham, 1989
OTO543M	Leyland Atlantean AN68/1R	East Lancashire	H47/26D	1974	Ex Nottingham, 1989
OTO549M	Leyland Atlantean AN68/1R	East Lancashire	H47/26D	1974	Ex Nottingham, 1990
OTO552M	Leyland Atlantean AN68/1R	East Lancashire	O47/33F	1974	Ex Nottingham, 1992
OTO571M	Leyland Atlantean AN68/1R	East Lancashire	H47/26D	1974	Ex Nottingham, 1989
SE4063-BU	Leyland Atlantean AN68/1R	East Lancashire	O47/32F	1974	Ex Nottingham, 1990
OTO573M	Leyland Atlantean AN68/1R	East Lancashire	O47/32F	1974	Ex Nottingham, 1989
OTO574M	Leyland Atlantean AN68/1R	East Lancashire	O47/32F	1974	Ex Nottingham, 1989
SE4064-BU	Leyland Atlantean AN68/1R	East Lancashire	O47/32F	1974	Ex Nottingham, 1989
OTO578M	Leyland Atlantean AN68/1R	East Lancashire	O47/32F	1974	Ex Nottingham, 1989
OTO582M	Leyland Atlantean AN68/1R	East Lancashire	O47/33F	1974	Ex Nottingham, 1992
SE0032-BX	Leyland Atlantean AN68/1R	East Lancashire	O47/32F	1974	Ex Nottingham, 1989
OTO584M	Leyland Atlantean AN68/1R	East Lancashire	O47/32F	1974	Ex Nottingham, 1989
OTO585M	Leyland Atlantean AN68/1R	East Lancashire	O47/32F	1974	Ex Nottingham, 1989
SE4065-BU	Leyland Atlantean AN68/1R	East Lancashire	O47/32F	1974	Ex Nottingham, 1990
GTO333N	Leyland Atlantean AN68/1R	East Lancashire	O47/32F	1975	Ex Nottingham, 1990

The lower front panel of OTO573M, seen on Waverley Bridge operating the Edinburgh Tour, gives a good indication of the many towns and cities where Guide Friday operates. The vehicle is one of a large batch of former Nottingham vehicles, several now converted to open top by their new owners, for use on specialised tours. Lettering for the location is used where possible.
Keith Grimes

WJY759 is one of the earliest Leyland Atlanteans built. Originally a Plymouth vehicle, it came to Guide Friday in 1991, though then to be found on the Plymouth tour. It has subsequently been transferred to, and lettered for, the Brighton tour. *Tim Weatherup*

Guide Friday tours with open toppers operate all year round in some towns. This photograph of OTO549M, also an East Lancashire-bodied Leyland Atlantean, was taken in Oxford in December 1993. Note the painted murals that are featured on many vehicles in this fleet. *Colin Lloyd*

GTO334N	Leyland Atlantean AN68/1R	East Lancashire	O47/32F	1975	Ex Nottingham, 1990
GTO335N	Leyland Atlantean AN68/1R	East Lancashire	O47/32F	1975	Ex Nottingham, 1990
SE4066-BU	Leyland Atlantean AN68/1R	East Lancashire	O47/32F	1975	Ex Nottingham, 1990
GRC888N	Leyland Atlantean AN68/1R	East Lancashire	O47/32F	1975	Ex Nottingham, 1989
GRC889N	Leyland Atlantean AN68/1R	East Lancashire	O47/32F	1975	Ex Nottingham, 1989
GRC890N	Leyland Atlantean AN68/1R	East Lancashire	O47/32F	1975	Ex Nottingham, 1990
GVO714N	Leyland Atlantean AN68/1R	East Lancashire	O47/31D	1975	Ex Nottingham, 1992
GVO715N	Leyland Atlantean AN68/1R(lpg)	East Lancashire	H47/31D	1975	Ex Nottingham, 1992
GVO716N	Leyland Atlantean AN68/1R	East Lancashire	O47/32F	1975	Ex Nottingham, 1990
GVO718N	Leyland Atlantean AN68/1R	East Lancashire	O47/32F	1975	Ex Nottingham, 1990
GVO719N	Leyland Atlantean AN68/1R	East Lancashire	O47/32F	1975	Ex Nottingham, 1990
<u>JAL876N</u>	Leyland Atlantean AN68/1R	East Lancashire	O47/31D	1975	Ex Nottingham, 1992
JAL880N	Leyland Atlantean AN68/1R	East Lancashire	H47/31D	1975	Ex Nottingham, 1992
KSU839P	Leyland Atlantean AN68/1R	Alexander	O45/31F	1975	Ex Windsorian, Windsor, 1990
MPT314P	Leyland Atlantean AN68/1R	Eastern Coach Works	O45/27D	1975	Ex Oxford Bus Company, 1992
MNV191P	Daimler Fleetline CRG6LX	Northern Counties	O47/32F	1976	Ex Nottingham, 1988
PAU196R	Daimler Fleetline CRG6LX	Northern Counties	O47/32F	1976	Ex Nottingham, 1989
PAU197R	Daimler Fleetline CRG6LX	Northern Counties	O47/32F	1976	Ex Nottingham, 1989
PAU198R	Daimler Fleetline CRG6LX	Northern Counties	O47/32F	1976	Ex Nottingham, 1989
PAU199R	Daimler Fleetline CRG6LX	Northern Counties	O47/32F	1976	Ex Nottingham, 1989
WWR417S	Bristol VRT/SL3/6LXB	Eastern Coach Works	O43/31F	1977	Ex York City & District, 1990
WWR418S	Bristol VRT/SL3/6LXB	Eastern Coach Works	O43/31F	1977	Ex York City & District, 1989
WWR419S	Bristol VRT/SL3/6LXB	Eastern Coach Works	O43/31F	1977	Ex York City & District, 1989
WWR420S	Bristol VRT/SL3/6LXB	Eastern Coach Works	O43/31F	1977	Ex York City & District, 1990
BKE861T	Bristol VRT/SL3/6LXB	Eastern Coach Works	O43/31F	1979	Ex Hastings & District, 1989

	Leyland Atlantean AN68/1R	Roe	O45/29D	1979	Ex South Yorkshire, 1991

566/7, 738/43/69 are H45/29D

CWF733T	CWF738T	CWG744V	CWG769V	DWJ566V
CWF736T	CWG743V	CWG763V	DWJ564V	DWJ567V

<u>KBU667V</u>	Leyland Leopard PSU3E/4R	Plaxton Supreme IV Express C53F	1980	Ex Duff, Sutton-on-the-Forest, 1993
GWV926V	Leyland Leopard PSU3E/4R	Plaxton Supreme IV Express C53F	1980	Ex Duff, Sutton-on-the-Forest, 1993

Previous Registrations:

SE0032-BX	OTO583M	SE4064-BU	OTO575M	SE4066-BU	GRC881N
SE4063-BU	OTO572M	SE4065-BU	GTO332N	XKO54A	620UKM

Livery: Cream and dark green

Unusually for a Guide Friday vehicle DWJ567V has a closed top! Such vehicles are required for the Edinburgh Airport bus service and the Coventry-Stratford service. This vehicle is a Roe-bodied Leyland Atlantean which came to Guide Friday in 1991 from South Yorkshire Transport.
Keith Grimes

HARRY SHAW

H Shaw (DM) Ltd, 44 Binley Road, Coventry
West Midlands, CV31 1JA

G892WFU	Mercedes-Benz 811D	Coachcraft	C24F	1990
G300XAC	Auwaerter Neoplan N122/3	Auwaerter Skyliner	CH57/20DT	1990
H5TGO	Mercedes-Benz 811D	Coachcraft	C24F	1991
84COV	Volvo B10M-60	Plaxton Paramount 3500 III	C53F	1991
3KOV	Kässbohrer Setra S215HD	Kässbohrer Tornado	C49FT	1992
KOV2	Kässbohrer Setra S215HD	Kässbohrer Tornado	C49FT	1992
J34UDU	Scania K113CRB	Plaxton Premiére 350	C49FT	1992
J35UHP	Scania K113TRB	Van Hool Astrobel	CH57/17CT	1992
J36UHP	Scania K113CRB	Plaxton Premiére 320	C53F	1992
J37UHP	Volvo B10M-60	Jonckheere Deauville P599	C51FT	1992
1KOV	Mercedes-Benz 0303	Plaxton Paramount 3500 III	C32FT	1992
K21GVC	Scania K113TRA	Van Hool Astrobel	CH57/17CT	1993
K23GVC	Scania K113TRB	Van Hool Alizée	C48FT	1993
K24GVC	Scania K113TRB	Van Hool Alizée	C48FT	1993
HST11	Volvo B10M-60	Plaxton Premiére 350	C49FT	1993
K27GVC	Volvo B10M-60	Plaxton Premiére 350	C49FT	1993
K28GVC	Volvo B10M-60	Plaxton Premiére 320	C53F	1993
K5URE	Scania K113TRB	Van Hool Alizée	C48FT	1993
L5URE	Scania K113CRB	Irizar Century	C49FT	1994
L19UER	Scania K113CRB	Irizar Century	C49FT	1994
L41VRW	Auwaerter Neoplan N122/3	Auwaerter Skyliner	CH57/22DT	1994
L42VRW	Volvo B10M-62	Plaxton Premiére 320	C57F	1994
L43VRW	Volvo B10M-62	Plaxton Premiére 320	C57F	1994
L45VRW	Volvo B10M-60	Plaxton Premiére 350	C53F	1994

Previous Registrations:

1KOV	J38WVC	84KOV	J31SDU	HST11	K26GVC
3KOV	J31UDU	H5TGO	J237LLB	KOV2	J32UDU

Livery: Orange, blue and white.

Harry Shaw's operation, based on Coventry, specialises in extended tours and holidays in Britain and on the Continent. A very up-to-date fleet is operated, with most vehicles remaining in the fleet for only 2-3 years. J36UHP is a Plaxton-bodied Scania K113 seen here either working a tour to the Irish Republic, or to the hit musical *Les Miserables* depending on which board you believe!.
Phillip Stephenson

HEYFORDIAN

Heyfordian Travel Ltd, Orchard Garage, Upper Heyford, Oxfordshire, OX6 3LP

Depots: March Place, Aylesbury; Lamarsh Road, Oxford, Orchard Lane, Upper Heyford and Downs Road, Witney.

FIL7662	Leyland Leopard PSU3A/4R	Plaxton Elite	C49F	1970	
FIL7661	Leyland Leopard PSU3B/4R	Plaxton Elite	C51F	1971	
FIL7663	Leyland Leopard PSU3B/4R	Plaxton Elite III	C53F	1972	Ex Jarvis, Middle Barton, 1973
FIL7664	Leyland Leopard PSU3B/4R	Plaxton Elite III	C53F	1972	Ex Ivins, Great Kingshill, 1986
3762KX	Volvo B58-56	Plaxton Elite III	C51F	1972	
2110UK	Leyland Leopard PSU5/4R	Plaxton Elite III	C53F	1975	
1636VB	AEC Reliance 6U2ZR	Plaxton Supreme III	C53F	1976	
FIL7297	Bedford YRQ	Plaxton Supreme III	C41F	1976	
FIL8446	Bedford YRQ	Plaxton Supreme III	C41F	1976	
FIL8317	Bedford YMT	Plaxton Supreme III Express	C53F	1976	Ex Hills, Tredegar, 1982
FIL8441	Bedford YMT	Plaxton Supreme III Express	C53F	1976	Ex Hills, Tredegar, 1982
FBZ7356	Bedford YMT	Plaxton Supreme III Express	C53F	1976	Ex Hills, Tredegar, 1982
9197WF	Bedford YMT	Plaxton Supreme III	C53F	1977	Ex King of the Road, Worthing, 1986
4128AP	AEC Reliance 6U2R	Plaxton Supreme III	C53F	1977	
1430PP	AEC Reliance 6U2R	Plaxton Supreme III	C53F	1977	
7209RU	AEC Reliance 6U2R	Plaxton Supreme III	C53F	1977	
3150MC	AEC Reliance 6U2R	Plaxton Supreme III	C53F	1977	
DFC884R	Bedford YMT	Plaxton Supreme III	C53F	1977	Ex Frostway, Upper Heyford, 1987
7298RU	Bedford YMT	Plaxton Supreme III	C53F	1978	Ex Premier, Watford, 1987
7223MY	Bedford YMT	Plaxton Supreme III	C53F	1978	Ex Smith, Rickmansworth, 1987
7396LJ	Bedford YMT	Plaxton Supreme III	C53F	1979	Ex Frostway, Upper Heyford, 1987

Passing through Parliament Square, in London, is Heyfordian's 3150MC, an AEC Reliance fitted with the full coach version of the Plaxton Supreme III body. Differences between the coach and express versions of this body are most obvious at the front. The express version, features a 'Bristol' dome and, of course, a two-piece door. *Colin Lloyd*

2462FD	AEC Reliance 6U2R	Duple Dominant II Express	C53F	1979	Ex London Country, 1985
7845LJ	AEC Reliance 6U2R	Duple Dominant II Express	C53F	1979	Ex London Country, 1985
7958NU	AEC Reliance 6U2R	Duple Dominant II Express	C53F	1979	Ex London Country, 1985
8252MX	AEC Reliance 6U2R	Duple Dominant II Express	C53F	1979	Ex London Country, 1985
8779KV	AEC Reliance 6U2R	Duple Dominant II Express	C53F	1979	Ex London Country, 1985
9945NE	AEC Reliance 6U2R	Duple Dominant II Express	C53F	1979	Ex London Country, 1985
HSV720	Bedford YMT	Plaxton Supreme IV	C53F	1979	Ex Premier, Watford, 1987
481HYE	Bedford YMT	Plaxton Supreme IV	C53F	1979	Ex Premier, Watford, 1987
VSF438	Bedford YMT	Plaxton Supreme IV	C53F	1981	Ex Smith, Rickmonsworth, 1987
748ECR	Bedford YMT	Plaxton Supreme IV	C53F	1981	Ex Smith, Rickmonsworth, 1987
943YKN	Bedford YMT	Plaxton Supreme IV	C53F	1981	Ex Smith, Rickmonsworth, 1987
FBZ7357	Bova EL26/581	Bova Europa	C49FT	1981	Ex Alder Valley South, 1991
3078RA	Bova EL26/581	Bova Europa	C53F	1982	Ex Staines Crusader, Clacton, 1984
4068MH	Bova EL26/581	Bova Europa	C53F	1982	Ex The Londoners, London SE15, 1987
YAY537	Bova EL26/581	Bova Europa	C53F	1982	Ex Chartercoach, Great Oakley, 1987
6940MD	Bova EL26/581	Bova Europa	C54F	1982	Ex The Londoners, London SE15, 1987
4078NU	Van Hool T815	Van Hool Acron	C40FT	1982	
3139KV	Bova EL26/581	Bova Europa	C53F	1983	Ex Wallace Arnold, 1987
6230NU	Bova EL26/581	Bova Europa	C53F	1983	Ex Wallace Arnold, 1987
2482NX	Bova EL26/581	Bova Europa	C53F	1983	Ex Wallace Arnold, 1987
2705TD	Bova EL26/581	Bova Europa	C41FT	1983	Ex Eastern National, 1987
PVV316	Bova EL26/581	Bova Europa	C52F	1983	Ex Tourmaster, Dunstable, 1987
5057VC	Bova EL26/581	Bova Europa	C53F	1983	
5701DP	Bova EL26/581	Bova Europa	C53F	1983	
2779UE	Bova EL26/581	Bova Europa	C53F	1983	Ex Grayline, Bicester, 1984
4827WD	Scania K112CRS	Jonckheere Jubilee P599	C51FT	1984	Ex BTS Borehamwood, 1991
HIL2295	Scania K112CRS	Jonckheere Jubilee P599	C49FT	1984	Ex Goodwin, Stockport, 1992
ESU940	Scania K112CRS	Jonckheere Jubilee P599	C51FT	1984	Ex Goodwin, Stockport, 1994
868AVO	Scania K112CRS	Jonckheere Jubilee P599	C51FT	1984	Ex Hardings, Huyton, 1992

Heyfordian have acquired several Scania coaches since two were purchased new in 1985 and, with the exception of 9467MU, these have Jonckheere Jubilee bodies. The exception, seen here in Coventry, carries a Berkhof Esprite body built at Valkenswaard in the Netherlands. *Colin Lloyd*

1264LG	Scania K112CRS	Jonckheere Jubilee P50	C53F	1985	
5089LG	Scania K112CRS	Jonckheere Jubilee P50	C53F	1985	
XCT550	Scania K112CRS	Jonckheere Jubilee P599	C51F	1985	Ex Cross Gates Coaches, 1992
6960TU	Scania K112CRS	Jonckheere Jubilee P599	C55F	1985	Ex Cresswell, Moira, 1991
2185NU	Bova EL29/581	Bova Europa	C53F	1985	Ex Tourmaster, Dunstable, 1987
8216FN	DAF SB2300DHS585	Plaxton Paramount 3200 II	C53F	1985	
9467MU	Scania K112CRB	Berkhof Esprite 350	C53F	1986	Ex West Kingsdown Coaches, 1992
LDZ2502	Scania K112CRB	Jonckheere Jubilee P599	C51FT	1987	Ex Buddens, Romsey, 1992
LDZ2503	Scania K112CRS	Jonckheere Jubilee P599	C51FT	1987	Ex Buddens, Romsey, 1992
HIL7403	Volvo B10M-61	Duple 340	C53F	1988	Ex Westbus, Ashford, 1993
8548VF	Volvo B10M-61	Duple 340	C53F	1988	Ex Westbus, Ashford, 1993
9769UK	Volvo B10M-61	Duple 340	C53F	1988	Ex Westbus, Ashford, 1993
9682FH	Volvo B10M-61	Duple 340	C53F	1988	Ex Westbus, Ashford, 1993
6595KV	Aüwaerter Neoplan N122/3	Aüwaerter Skyliner	CH57/20DT	1989	Ex Voyager, Selby, 1992
2622NU	Toyota Coaster HB31R	Caetano Optimo	C21F	1990	
1435VZ	Hestair Duple SDA1512	Duple 425	C57F	1990	Ex Limebourne, London SW8, 1994
L535XUT	Toyota Coaster HZB50R	Caetano Optimo III	C18F	1994	
L26CAY	MAN 10-190	Caetano Algarve II	C33FT	1994	

Previous Registrations:

1264LG	B157YBW	5701DP	From new	9945NE	YPL103T
1430PP	XWL801R	6230NU	FUA396Y	ESU490	A60JLW
1435VZ	G648YVS	6595KV	F625OWJ, NIW2235	FBZ7356	MHB854P, 4827WD, UFC144P
1636VB	PUD371P	6940MD	YMV351Y	FBZ7357	KEP640X
2110UK	KBW118N	6960TU	B71MLT, C47CKR	FIL7297	SUD464P
2185NU	B246YKX	7209RU	XWL798R	FIL7661	AUD310J
2462FD	YPL67T	7223MY	CMJ99T	FIL7662	VUD384H
2482NX	FUA398Y	7298RU	CMJ3T	FIL7663	YWL134K
2622NU	G152ELJ	7396LJ	YOG965T	FIL7664	CJH615K
2705TD	BGX649Y	748ECR	UNK101W	FIL8317	MHB852P
2779UE	FWL782Y	7845LJ	YPL84T	FIL8441	MHB853P
3078RA	DEV807X	7958NU	YPL73T	FIL8446	SUD465P
3139KV	FUA395Y	8216FN	From new	HIL2295	A131XNH
3150MC	XWL799R	8252MK	YPL61T	HIL7403	E172OMU
3762KX	LBW185L	8548VF	E173OMU	HSV720	KPP8V
4068MH	JAB311X	868AVO	A52JLW	LDZ2502	D313VVV
4078NU	From new	8779KV	YPL77T	LDZ2503	D312VVV
4128AP	XWL800R	9197WF	SJU227R	PVV316	JRO615Y
481HYE	KPP9V	943YKN	UNK102W	VSF438	KPP100V
4827WD	A59JLW, ESU930, A545TMU	9467MU	C829LJN	XCT550	B504CBD, HYY3, B984MAB
5057VC	From new	9682FH	E175OMU	YAY537	GGJ341X
5089LG	B156YBW	9769UK	E174OMU		

Livery: Off-white, orange, red and yellow

The long list of re-registrations above typifies the growing trend for changes in marks especially away from the standard annual series. Though carrying 2462FD the keen enthusiast will quickly recognise one of the many former London County Duple Dominant-bodied AEC Reliances. Originally RB67 the vehicle is seen at Great Missenden. Disposal of this batch commenced recently. *Colin Lloyd*

HI RIDE

F Pellington, 60 Holly Road, Handsworth, Birmingham,
West Midlands, B20 2DB

PTF226M	Leyland Leopard PSU3B/4R	Duple Dominant	C53F	1974	Ex Drayton Vale, Ratby, 1991
JHA207L	Leyland Leopard PSU3B/2R	Marshall	DP49F	1973	Ex Enterprise & Silver Dawn, 1992
PTF226M	Leyland Leopard PSU3B/4R	Duple Dominant	C53F	1974	Ex Drayton Vale, Ratby, 1991
GWY691N	Leyland Leopard PSU4B/2R	Plaxton Derwent	B43F	1975	Ex Glyn Williams, Crosskeys, 1993
JOX451P	Leyland Leopard PSU3C/4R	Plaxton Supreme III	C48F	1976	Ex Perry, Bromyard, 1992
OJD60R	Bristol LH6L	Eastern Coach Works	B39F	1977	ExPerry, Bromyard, 1992

Livery: White, red and green

Previously with Glynn Williams of Cross Keys GWY691N is an example of the shorter version
Leyland Leopard favoured by many operators in the 1960s and early 1970s for rural operation. Fitted
with a Plaxton Derwent body, it is seen working Hi Ride's service 40X to Bearwood. *Tim Weatherup*

HOLLANDS

G A Mole, Crossley Estate, Mill Street, Kidderminster,
Hereford & Worcester, DY11 3XG

OHA436W	Ford Transit 190	Reeve Burgess	C17F	1981	Ex Mini-Mac, Kippax, 1989
KGE299Y	Ford Transit 190	Dormobile	M16	1983	Ex More, Greenock, 1989
D392KND	Ford Transit VE6	Mellor	M16	1986	Ex Owen, Kidderminster, 1991
D723JUB	Freight Rover Sherpa	Carlyle	B16F	1986	Ex Horrocks, Brockton, 1993
D247OOJ	Freight Rover Sherpa	Carlyle	B20F	1987	Ex Victoria Shuttle, London, 1991
D133NON	Freight Rover Sherpa	Carlyle	B20F	1987	Ex Bee Line Buzz, 1991
D118TFT	Freight Rover Sherpa	Carlyle	B18F	1987	Ex Merry Hill Minibus, 1991

Livery: White and blue

Some Kidderminster local services are operated by Hollands using four Freight Rovers. **D118TFT** was one of a large batch of Carlyle-bodied vehicles supplied to Tyne and Wear (Busways) in 1986/87, which are now dispersed all over the country. **D118TFT** is about to take up service on the Cookley route. *Phillip Stephenson*

JEFFS

Jeffs Coaches Ltd, Suite 1, Windrush Court, 56a High Street, Witney,
Oxfordshire, OX8 6HJ
JV & K R Jeffs, Old Station Yard, Helmdon, Brackley, Northamptonshire, NN13 5QT
Payne's Coaches & Car Hire Ltd, Old Station Yard, Helmdon, Brackley,
Northamptonshire, NN13 5QT
Basford's Coaches Ltd, The Dingle, High Street, Greens Norton,
Northamptonshire, NN12 8BA
Silverline Travel Ltd, Main Road Garage, Middleton Cheney, Northamptonshire

W	OTA293G	Bristol VRT/SL2/6G	Eastern Coach Works	H39/31F	1969	Ex Windrush Valley Coaches, 1990
W	WCD519K	Bristol VRT/SL2/6G	Eastern Coach Works	H39/31F	1971	Ex Windrush Valley Coaches, 1990
B	ERP2K	Leyland Leopard PSU3E/4R	Plaxton Elite II Express	C53F	1972	Ex Basford's Cs, Greens Norton, 1987
P	LNV564P	Bedford YRT	Duple Dominant	C53F	1972	Ex Paynes Coaches, Buckingham, 1986
W	LHK88P	Bedford YRQ	Duple Dominant	C45F	1975	Ex Windrush Valley Coaches, 1990
B	MNH3P	Ford R1114	Duple Dominant	C53F	1976	Ex Basford's Cs, Greens Norton, 1987
B	NDU765P	Ford R1114	Duple Dominant	C53F	1976	Ex Basford's Cs, Greens Norton, 1987
W	NFX447P	Bedford YMT	Plaxton Supreme III	C53F	1976	Ex Windrush Valley Coaches, 1990
H	PNV957R	Bedford YMT	Duple Dominant II	C53F	1976	
H	647PJO	Leyland Leopard PSU5A/4R	Plaxton Supreme III	C50F	1976	Ex Percival's, Oxford, 1987
H	AUD465R	Bristol VRT/SL3/501	Eastern Coach Works	H43/31F	1976	Ex Oxford Bus Company, 1993
H	CJO466R	Bristol VRT/SL3/501	Eastern Coach Works	H43/31F	1976	Ex Oxford Bus Company, 1993
W	ADC277A	Bedford YLQ	Plaxton Supreme III	C45F	1977	Ex Windrush Valley Coaches, 1990
P	XYG909S	Ford R1114	Plaxton Supreme III	C53F	1977	Ex Payne's Coaches, Buckingham, 1986
H	279JJO	Leyland Leopard PSU5A/4R	Plaxton Supreme III	C57F	1977	Ex Percival's, Oxford, 1987
H	VVV66S	Bristol VRT/SL3/6LXB	Alexander AL	H45/27D	1977	Ex Northampton, 1991
H	VRP45S	Bristol VRT/SL3/6LXB	Alexander AL	H45/27D	1978	Ex Northampton, 1991
H	VRP51S	Bristol VRT/SL3/6LXB	Alexander AL	H45/27D	1978	Ex Northampton, 1991
H	VYU758S	Bedford YMT	Duple Dominant II	C53F	1978	Ex Percival's, Oxford, 1987
H	VBW846	Leyland Leopard PSU5C/4R	Plaxton Supreme III	C55F	1978	Ex Percival's, Oxford, 1987
H	5615RO	Leyland Leopard PSU3E/4R	Duple Dominant II	C49F	1978	Ex Percival's, Oxford, 1987
H	WVV826S	Bedford YMT	Duple Dominant II	C53F	1978	
H	WVV827S	Bedford YMT	Duple Dominant II	C53F	1978	
B	WVV829S	Bedford YMT	Duple Dominant II	C53F	1978	
B	WVV830S	Bedford YMT	Duple Dominant II	C53F	1978	
H	WVV832S	Bedford YMT	Duple Dominant II	C53F	1978	
H	FDF276T	Leyland Leopard PSU5C/4R	Plaxton Supreme IV	C57F	1979	
P	FDU6T	Bedford YMT	Plaxton Supreme IV	C53F	1979	Ex Payne's Coaches, Buckingham, 1986
W	VNP893	Leyland Leopard PSU3E/4R	Plaxton Supreme IV	C53F	1979	Ex Windrush Valley Coaches, 1990
H	ERP19T	Leyland Leopard PSU5C/4R	Duple Dominant II	C53F	1979	

This Bedford YMT with Duple bodywork was new to Basford of Greens Norton, Northamptonshire in February 1980. The vehicle remained in that fleet when control passed to Jeffs of Helmdon. Jeffs expanded into the sphere of this book through the acquisition of Windrush Valley Coaches in 1990.

W	YFC16V	Leyland Leopard PSU3E/4R	Duple Dominant II Express	C49F	1979	Ex Windrush Valley Coaches, 1990
W	YFC17V	Leyland Leopard PSU3E/4R	Duple Dominant II Express	C49F	1979	Ex Windrush Valley Coaches, 1990
H	MDS228V	Volvo B58-61	Duple Dominant II Express	C49F	1979	Ex Windrush Valley Coaches, 1990
H	GDG442V	Leyland Leopard PSU3E/4R	Plaxton Supreme IV Express	C53F	1979	Ex Pulhams, Bourton-on-the-Water, 1991
W	EYH809V	Leyland Leopard PSU3E/4R	Duple Dominant II	C49F	1980	Ex Windrush Valley Coaches, 1990
H	NBD304V	Bedford YMT	Duple Dominant II	C53F	1980	
H	NBD305V	Bedford YMT	Duple Dominant II	C53F	1980	
H	NBD306V	Bedford YMT	Duple Dominant II	C53F	1980	
H	NBD307V	Bedford YMT	Duple Dominant II	C53F	1980	
H	NBD309V	Bedford YMT	Duple Dominant II	C53F	1980	
B	NBD310V	Bedford YMT	Duple Dominant II	C53F	1980	
B	NBD311V	Bedford YMT	Duple Dominant II	C53F	1980	
H	195JOH	Volvo B58-61	Jonckheere Bermuda	C53F	1980	
H	938HNM	Volvo B10M-61	Jonckheere Bermuda	C51F	1981	
H	ESU635	Volvo B10M-61	Jonckheere Bermuda	C51F	1981	
H	FSV720	Volvo B10M-61	Jonckheere Bermuda	C51F	1981	
B	TGY698	Volvo B10M-61	Jonckheere Bermuda	C51F	1981	
B	VKX510	Volvo B10M-61	Jonckheere Bermuda	C52F	1981	
H	802AOJ	Volvo B10M-61	Jonckheere Bermuda	C49FT	1981	
P	WRP643W	Ford A0609	Moseley Faro	DP25F	1981	Ex Payne's Coaches, Buckingham, 1986
H	382PCV	Volvo B10M-61	Jonckheere Bermuda	C50FT	1982	
H	872KMY	Volvo B58-61	Jonckheere Bermuda	C51FT	1982	
P	GNV499X	Ford R1114	Plaxton Supreme V	C53F	1982	Ex Payne's Coaches, Buckingham, 1986
H	VXT571	Volvo B10M-61	Jonckheere Jubilee P50	C49FT	1983	
H	112AXN	Volvo B10M-61	Jonckheere Jubilee P50	C49FT	1983	
H	147VKN	Volvo B10M-61	Jonckheere Jubilee P50	C51FT	1984	
H	XWG254	Volvo B10M-61	Jonckheere Jubilee P50	C51FT	1984	
H	YSV815	Volvo B10M-61	Jonckheere Jubilee P50	C53F	1984	
B	487VYA	Volvo B10M-61	Jonckheere Jubilee P50	C53FT	1984	Ex Basford's Cs, Greens Norton, 1987

Photographed at Banbury on tendered service 510 is Jeffs MDS228V, a Volvo B58 with Duple Dominant II bodywork. The head office of the group is in Northamptonshire and considerable expansion, through acquisition, has occurred in recent years. *Keith Grimes*

W	1576CD	DAF SB2305DHTD585	Plaxton Paramount 3200	C53F	1984	Ex Dore, Leafield, 1993
W	3493CD	Volvo B10M-61	Plaxton Paramount 3200 II	C53F	1985	Ex Dore, Leafield, 1993
W	B109XJO	Ford Transit 190	Carlyle	DP16F	1985	Ex Windrush Valley Coaches, 1990
W	B702GJR	Volvo B10M-61	Duple Laser	C55F	1985	Ex Windrush Valley Coaches, 1990
W	B530BJO	DAF MB200DKFL600	Plaxton Paramount 3500 II	C53F	1985	Ex Dore, Leafield, 1993
W	C681CNF	Freight Rover Sherpa	Made-to-Measure	M16	1986	Ex Willoughby & Harris, Freeland, 1993
W	D315MNC	Freight Rover Sherpa	Made-to-Measure	M16	1987	Ex Willoughby & Harris, Freeland, 1993
S	E81HPG	Mercedes-Benz 811D	Plaxton Mini Supreme	C19F	1988	Ex Silverline, Middleton Cheney, 1993
W	E764HJF	Volvo B10M-61	Caetano Algarve	C53F	1988	Ex Windrush Valley Coaches, 1990
W	E741DJO	Volvo B10M-61	Plaxton Paramount 3500 III	C53F	1988	Ex Dore, Leafield, 1993
W	F567HPP	Ford Transit VE6	Chassis Developments	M16	1988	Ex Willoughby & Harris, Freeland, 1993
B	F201PNR	Volvo B10M-60	Caetano Algarve	C49FT	1989	
B	F202PNR	Volvo B10M-60	Caetano Algarve	C49FT	1989	
H	F203PNR	Volvo B10M-60	Caetano Algarve	C53F	1989	
H	F204PNR	Volvo B10M-60	Caetano Algarve	C53F	1989	
H	F205PNR	Volvo B10M-60	Caetano Algarve	C53F	1989	
H	F206PNR	Volvo B10M-60	Caetano Algarve	C53F	1989	
P	F47CVV	Mercedes-Benz 811D	Optare StarRider	DP33F	1989	
P	F48CVV	Mercedes-Benz 811D	Optare StarRider	DP33F	1989	
W	F480AKC	Mercedes-Benz 609D	North West CS	C24F	1989	Ex Windrush Valley Coaches, 1990
W	ESU974	LAG G355Z	LAG Panoramic	C49FT	1989	Ex Dore, Leafield, 1993
H	G965VBC	Toyota Coaster HB31R	Caetano Optimo	C19F	1989	
W	G933JKY	Leyland DAF 400	Crystals	M16	1989	Ex Willoughby & Harris, Freeland, 1993
W	G956VVR	Ford Transit VE6	Steedrive	M16	1990	Ex Willoughby & Harris, Freeland, 1993
H	G907WAY	Volvo B10M-60	Caetano Algarve	C53F	1990	
H	G908WAY	Volvo B10M-60	Caetano Algarve	C53F	1990	
H	G909WAY	Volvo B10M-60	Caetano Algarve	C53F	1990	
P	G910WAY	Volvo B10M-60	Caetano Algarve	C53F	1990	
B	G911WAY	Volvo B10M-60	Caetano Algarve	C53F	1990	
S	G912WAY	Volvo B10M-60	Caetano Algarve	C53F	1990	
H	G913WAY	Volvo B10M-60	Caetano Algarve	C53F	1990	
H	G914WAY	Volvo B10M-60	Caetano Algarve	C53F	1990	
H	H409CJF	Toyota Coaster HDB30R	Caetano Optimo	C21F	1990	
H	H183EJF	Volvo B10M-60	Caetano Algarve	C49FT	1991	
H	H184EJF	Volvo B10M-60	Caetano Algarve	C49FT	1991	
P	J520LRY	Dennis Javelin 12SDA1919	Caetano Algarve II	C53F	1991	
P	J521LRY	Dennis Javelin 12SDA1919	Caetano Algarve II	C53F	1991	
S	J470NJU	Toyota Coaster HDB30R	Caetano Optimo II	C18F	1992	
P	J471NJU	Toyota Coaster HDB30R	Caetano Optimo II	C18F	1992	
H	J472NJU	Volvo B10M-60	Caetano Algarve II	C49FT	1992	
H	J473NJU	Volvo B10M-60	Caetano Algarve II	C49FT	1992	
H	J474NJU	Volvo B10M-60	Caetano Algarve II	C49FT	1992	
H	J475NJU	Volvo B10M-60	Caetano Algarve II	C49FT	1992	
H	J476NJU	Volvo B10M-60	Caetano Algarve II	C49FT	1992	
H	J477NJU	Volvo B10M-60	Caetano Algarve II	C49FT	1992	
H	K698RNR	Volvo B6	Caetano Algarve II	C35F	1993	
H	K699RNR	Volvo B6	Caetano Algarve II	C35F	1993	
H	K97UFP	Dennis Javelin 12SDA2101	Caetano Algarve II	C57F	1993	
H	K98UFP	Dennis Javelin 12SDA2101	Caetano Algarve II	C57F	1993	

Previous Registrations:

112AXN	NNV607Y	647PJO	SGN331R	FSV720	XNV143W
147VKN	A591XRP	802AOJ	BBD851X	TGY698	XNV144W
1576CD	A875PJX	872KMY	DVV528X	VBW846	CGF311S
195JOH	PBD776V	938HNM	XNV140W	VKX510	XNV145W
279JJO	SUR286R	ADC277A	PKU621R	VNP893	EWW206T
3493CD	B531BML	B530BJO	B878AJX, 3600CD, 1991CD	VXT571	NNV606Y
382PCV	DVV529X	E741DJO	E665UNE, 6504CD	XWG254	A592XRP
487VYA	A594XRP	ESU635	XNV142W	YSV815	A593XRP
5615RO	XWX183S	ESU974	F121LUD, 9119CD		

Livery: White, red and green.

Note: The allocation of vehicles to subsidiaries is indicated by: W - Jeff's, Witney; B - Basford's; P - Payne's; H - Jeff's, Helmdon and S - Silverline.

One early example of the shorter version of the Caetano Algarve II body has been fitted to a pair of Volvo B6s for Jeffs who have been loyal Caetano customers for several years. Though allocated to Helmdon, K699RNR is seen arriving in Banbury. *Keith Grimes*

ERP2K is seen here in Mid Summer Boulevard in Milton Keynes, working a Buckingham-Milton Keynes service. This vehicle was new to Basfords in 1972 and is a Plaxton-bodied Leyland Leopard.

KEN ROSE

Ken Rose Coaches (Broadway) Ltd, Cheltenham Road, Broadway
Hereford and Worcester, WR12 7BZ

VUR896W	Volvo B58-61	Duple Dominant IV	C57F	1981	Ex Travel Line, Abbots Langley, 1994
UWA579Y	Ford R1114	Duple Dominant IV	C53F	1983	Ex Stevens, Bristol, 1992
D957WJH	Freight Rover Sherpa	Dormobile	B16F	1986	Ex Hampshire Bus, 1992
D869BDG	Ford Transit 190	Dormobile	M16	1987	Ex RCJ Hire, Winchcombe, 1992
F536DWE	Mercedes-Benz 609D	Reeve Burgess Beaver	C25F	1988	
F146UFH	Leyland DAF 400	Leyland DAF	M16	1989	Ex Brimm, Honeybourne, 1992
F130TDF	Hestair Duple SDA1512	Duple 425	C51FT	1989	Ex Swanbrook, Cheltenham, 1994
K736PAB	Mercedes-Benz 711D	Plaxton Beaver	C25F	1993	

Previous Registrations:

6837KR	C530DND	VUR896W	PDJ903W, FSU386

Livery: White

Ken Rose Coaches operate stage services and tours from a base in the picturesque Cotswold village of Broadway. While the latest addition to the fleet is a former Swanbrook Hestair Duple 425, and still to be found in that operators colours, the stage requirement is met by the minibuses. K736PAB is a Mercedes-Benz 711D with Reeve Burgess Beaver bodywork and fitted with high-back seating.
Bill Potter

LIONSPEED

Lionspeed Ltd, Somerset House, Temple Street, Birmingham, West Midlands, B2 5DN

Depot: Unit 47, Imex Business Park, Bordesley Green Road, Birmingham.

D822PUK	Freight Rover Sherpa	Carlyle	B18F	1987	Ex Bentley, Birmingham, 1993
D828PUK	Freight Rover Sherpa	Carlyle	B18F	1987	Ex Bentley, Birmingham, 1993
D225OOJ	Freight Rover Sherpa	Carlyle	B18F	1987	Ex Harrisons, Blackburn, 1994
E87OUH	Freight Rover Sherpa	Carlyle Citybus 2	B20F	1987	Ex Shamrock, Pontypridd, 1993
F233BAX	Freight Rover Sherpa	Carlyle Citybus 2	B20F	1988	Ex Harrisons, Blackburn, 1994
F889XOE	Freight Rover Sherpa	Carlyle Citybus 2	B20F	1988	Ex The Wright Company, 1994
F895XOE	Freight Rover Sherpa	Carlyle Citybus 2	B20F	1988	Ex The Wright Company, 1994

Livery: Green and yellow

Lionspeed took over a local service of Careline in Birmingham in August 1993. The current, seven-vehicle fleet consists entirely of Freight Rovers. C738HKK is a Dormobile-bodied example with 16 seats recently replaced by further examples with Carlyle Cutybus 2 bodywork. It was photographed outside the Sainsbury supermarket in Shirley, to the south of the Birmingham shortly before its withdrawal. *Tim Weatherup*

LITTLE RED BUS

Little Red Bus Co Ltd, 89 Rabone Lane, Smethwick, West Midlands, B66 3JJ

EX9779	AEC Reliance	Duple Britannia	C41C	1956	Ex Staniforth, Birmingham, 1993
XHA875	Bedford YRQ	Duple Dominant	C45F	1974	Ex Evans, Tregaron, 1993
OAH106	Bedford YRQ	Plaxton Elite III	C45F	1975	Ex Melksham Coaches, 1994
SAD700N	Bedford YRQ	Plaxton Elite III	C45F	1975	Ex Melksham Coaches, 1994
891EHA	Bedford YRQ	Plaxton Elite III	C45F	1975	Ex Melksham Coaches, 1993
B453WTC	Ford Transit 190	Dormobile	B16F	1985	Ex John's Travel, Nantyglo, 1993
C505BFB	Ford Transit 190	Dormobile	B16F	1986	Ex Warleigh, Bradford on Avon, 1993
C819CBU	Renault-Dodge S56	Northern Counties	B18F	1986	Ex G M Buses, 1991
C822CBU	Renault-Dodge S56	Northern Counties	B18F	1986	Ex G M Buses, 1991
C838CBU	Renault-Dodge S56	Northern Counties	B18F	1986	Ex G M Buses, 1991
D107OWG	Renault-Dodge S56	Reeve Burgess Beaver	B25F	1987	Ex South Yorkshire, 1991
D707TWM	Renault-Dodge S56	Northern Counties	B22F	1987	Ex Merseybus, 1993
D712TWM	Renault-Dodge S56	Northern Counties	B22F	1987	Ex Merseybus, 1993
D715TWM	Renault-Dodge S56	Northern Counties	B22F	1987	Ex Merseybus, 1993
YHA116	Bedford YMQ	Plaxton Paramount 3200 III	C35F	1987	Ex McLaughlin, Penwortham, 1994
E635DCK	Renault-Dodge S56	Dormobile	B25F	1987	Ex United Counties, 1993
E638DCK	Renault-Dodge S56	Dormobile	B25F	1987	Ex United Counties, 1993
E639DCK	Renault-Dodge S56	Dormobile	B25F	1987	Ex United Counties, 1993
E641DCK	Renault-Dodge S56	Dormobile	B25F	1987	Ex Fife Scottish, 1993
E645DCK	Renault-Dodge S56	Dormobile	B25F	1987	Ex United Counties, 1993

Previous Registrations:

891EHA	HRD13N	OHA106	SDD108N	YHA116	D793SGB, FTG5, D949CFR
EX9779	From new	XHA875	TOT245M, NKH319, PDE87M		

Livery: Red

The Little Red Bus Company started to run local services in August 1991 and for the first year of its operation ran only minibuses - so the company title was appropriate. The first larger vehicle arrived in August 1992. 891EHA is a Plaxton-bodied Bedford YRQ new in 1975 and originally registered HRD13N. Three of the larger vehicles carry HA registrations which are apt, as the company is based in Smethwick.
Tim Weatherup

Most of the minibuses in the fleet are Renault-Dodge S56 models. E641DCK and five others came from within the Stagecoach group and have Dormobile bodies. Others have come from Merseyside and Greater Manchester. *Tim Weatherup*

In contrast to the Dormobile example above, the Northern Counties version is represented by C822CBU, another Renault-Dodge S56 chassis, and one of a large delivery made to G M Buses in the mid 1980s. Little Red Bus' AEC Reliance/Duple Britannia will be carrying out a long distance (Smethwick- John O'Groats - Lands End) journey during the summer of 1994 to raise money for charity.
Tim Weatherup

LLOYDS

J Lloyd & Son Ltd, Avenue Road, Nuneaton, Warwickshire, CV11 4JN

NDU998P	Bedford YLQ	Plaxton Supreme III Express	C45F	1976	
RAW45R	Bedford YLQ	Duple Dominant II	C45F	1977	Ex Chartercoach, Great Oakley, 1991
SDG650R	Bedford YMT	Plaxton Supreme III	C53F	1977	Ex Nash, Nuneaton, 1990
UDW141S	Bedford YMT	Plaxton Supreme III Express	C53F	1978	Ex Terry Field, Balby, 1991
XDU997S	Bedford YMT	Plaxton Supreme III Express	C53F	1978	
XDU998S	Bedford YMT	Plaxton Supreme III Express	C53F	1978	
XAK456T	Leyland National 11351A/1R		B52F	1978	Ex Yorkshire Tracetion, 1990
XAK457T	Leyland National 11351A/1R		B52F	1978	Ex Yorkshire Tracetion, 1990
YMU134	Leyland Leopard PSU3E/4R	Plaxton Supreme III	C50F	1978	Ex Donald, Brook, 1992
GGT335T	Leyland Leopard PSU5C/4R	Plaxton Supreme IV	C50F	1979	Ex Epsom Coaches, 1993
EAC877T	Bedford YMT	Plaxton Supreme IV Express	C53F	1979	
EAC878T	Bedford YMT	Plaxton Supreme IV Express	C53F	1979	
FDU807T	Bedford YMT	Plaxton Supreme IV Express	C53F	1979	
PGC340V	Leyland Leopard PSU5C/4R	Plaxton Supreme IV	C50F	1980	Ex Epsom Coaches, 1993
WCO732V	Volvo B58-61	Caetano Alpha	C53F	1980	Ex Nash, Nuneaton, 1990
UNK10W	Bedford YMT	Plaxton Supreme IV	C53F	1981	Ex Smith, Corby Glen, 1992
MPL332W	Bedford YMT	Unicar	C53F	1981	Ex Briscoe, Milford, 1988
EVC257Y	Bedford YMT	Plaxton Paramount 3200 E	C53F	1983	
B224OJU	Bedford YNV Venturer	Duple Laser	C57F	1985	Ex Moor-Dale, Newcastle, 1991
C399FBO	Bedford YNT	Duple Laser 2	C53F	1986	Ex Capitol, Cwmbran, 1991
DJI2517	Bedford YNT	Plaxton Paramount 3200 II	C50F	1985	Ex Capitol, Cwmbran, 1987
D259FRW	Bedford YNV Venturer	Duple 320	C57F	1987	
DJI5578	Volvo B10M-61	Van Hool Alizée	C49FT	1987	Ex Cambridge Coach Services, 1992
DJI8467	Volvo B10M-61	Caetano Algarve	C49FT	1988	Ex Spirit of London, Hounslow, 1992
F207EWN	DAF SB2305DHS585	Caetano Algarve	C49FT	1989	Ex D Coaches, Morriston, 1993
G839VAY	Dennis Javelin 12SDA1907	Caetano Algarve	C53F	1989	

Previous Registrations:

DJI2517	B609DDW	DJI8467	E232EFW
DJI5578	D847KVE	YMU134	WOC728T

Livery: Blue and white

Photographed outside their offices on Nuneaton bus station is ECA877T, one of several Bedford YMTs in the Lloyds fleet most of which carry Plaxton Supreme bodies. *Bill Potter*

LUDLOWS

Ludlows of Halesowen Ltd, 239 Stourbridge Road, Halesowen,
West Midlands, B63 3QU

Depots: Quarry Road, Cradley Heath

ABW210L	Leyland National 1151/1R/0401	B52F	1973	Ex Tappins, Didcot, 1992
NPD111L	Leyland National 1151/2R/0402	B46F	1973	Ex City Line, 1989
NAT222A	Leyland National 1151/1R/0402	B49F	1973	Ex Eastern National, 1989
NAT333A	Leyland National 1051/1R/0502	B44F	1973	Ex Southern Vectis, 1987
NAT555A	Leyland National 1151/1R/0401	B52F	1973	Ex Eastern National, 1989
PVT244L	Leyland National 1151/1R/0401	B52F	1973	Ex PMT, 1991
WNO556L	Leyland National 1151/1R/0401	B52F	1973	Ex Eastern National, 1989
RFM886M	Leyland National 1151/1R	B49F	1974	Ex Crosville, 1987
ORP466M	Leyland National 1151/1R	B49F	1974	Ex United Counties, 1988
TPD195M	Leyland National 1051/1R	B41F	1974	Ex Southend, 1992
UPE199M	Leyland National 1051/1R	B41F	1974	Ex Southend, 1992
GHU645N	Leyland National 10351/1R	B44F	1975	Ex Southend, 1992
KCR108P	Leyland National 10351/1R	B40D	1977	Ex Orion, Kirkcaldy, 1993

Ludlows have two Dennis Darts with Carlyle bodywork which were purchased new. The second of these is J272SOC which seats 43 . They are normally used on the Romsley service, although lettered on the side for Service 002 which connects south west Birmingham with the huge Merry Hill Shopping Centre at Brierley Hill. *Phillip Stephenson*

OFD231P	Leyland National 11351/1R		B50F	1977	Ex Athelstan, Malmesbury, 1989
PTT80R	Leyland National 11351A/1R		B52F	1977	Ex Athelstan, Malmesbury, 1989
VPT596R	Leyland National 11351A/1R		B49F	1978	Ex Tyneside, 1992
NWO460R	Leyland National 11351/1R/SC (Volvo)		DP48F	1978	Ex Rhondda, 1994
JBR690T	Leyland National 10351A/1R		B49F	1979	Ex United, 1993
BOK62T	Leyland Leopard PSU3E/4R	Plaxton Supreme IV	C53F	1979	Ex Rover Coaches, Horsley, 1992
DSJ307V	Volvo B58-56	Duple Dominant II	C53F	1980	Ex Arvonia, Llanrug, 1992
8797PL	Volvo B10M-61	Van Hool Alizée	C53F	1984	Ex Shearings, 1989
YWD687	Leyland TRCTL11/3R	Duple Laser	C51F	1985	Ex Safeguard, Guildford, 1992
GJI2223	Volvo B10M-61	Duple Caribbean 2	C49FT	1986	Ex Swanbrook, Cheltenham, 1991
SXD696	Volvo B10M-61	Van Hool Alizée	C53F	1986	Ex Shearings, 1991
1223PL	Volvo B10M-61	Ikarus Blue Danube	C53F	1989	Ex Alexanders, Aberdeen, 1990
H720LOL	Dennis Dart 9SDL3002	Carlyle Dartline	B36F	1990	
J272SOC	Dennis Dart 9.8SDL3004	Carlyle Dartline	B43F	1991	

Previous Registrations:

1223PL	F108SSE	NAT222A	KCG610L	
8797PL	A192MNE	NAT333A	XDL802L	
ABW210L	LWN713L, 653GBU	OFD231P	NAT555A	WNO551L
BOK62T	CTM413T, YWD687	MOD818P, CSU992		
GJI2223	C118XDD	SXD696	C535DND	
KCR108P	KCR108P, 2704MAN	YWD687	B717MPC	

Livery: White; Blue, yellow, white and red (Coaches).

SXD696 is one of Ludlows' private marks and has been on several vehicles in the fleet, though it is normally carried by the current premier coach. In this photograph it is on a Volvo B10M with Van Hool bodywork that came from Shearings in 1992 and was photographed while attending last year's Brighton Coach Rally. *Ivor Norman*

Ludlows' Leyland Nationals are eye-catching in their all-white livery, particularly if they carry the type of advertisement seen here. NAT222A is a very early Leyland National. It was new in 1973 as KCG610L to Alder Valley, having formed part of the Aldershot and District allocation from NBC, and later passed to Eastern National. It has been with Ludlows for five years. *Phillip Stephenson*

Another example of Leyland National can be seen in PVT244L, an early example from PMT. The vehicle is seen in Halesowen while heading for Harborne. *Roy Marshall*

LUGG VALLEY

Miss D J Staples, 131 Etnam Street, Leominster, Hereford & Worcester, HR6 8AF

Depots: Station Yard Industrial Estate, Leominster.

JCJ800E	Bedford VAM5	Duple Viceroy	C45F	1967	Ex Yeomans, Hereford, 1970
VEN416L	Bedford YRT	Duple Dominant	C53F	1973	Ex Elsworth, Blackpool, 1975
NCJ800M	Bedford YRQ	Duple Dominant Express	C45F	1973	Ex Yeomans, Hereford, 1978
PVJ300M	Bedford YRQ	Duple Dominant	C45F	1974	Ex Canyon, Hereford, 1980
MHB855P	Bedford YLQ	Plaxton Supreme III Express	C45F	1976	Ex Hills, Tredegar, 1988
MCJ900P	Bedford YLQ	Plaxton Supreme III Express	C45F	1976	
DJS203	Bedford YRT	Duple Dominant	C53F	1976	Ex Waterhouse, Polegate, 1979
OVJ700R	Bedford YLQ	Plaxton Supreme III Express	C45F	1976	
NUY312T	Bedford YLQ	Plaxton Supreme IV	C45F	1976	Ex Rover, Bromsgrove, 1989
BFO400V	Bedford YMT	Plaxton Supreme IV Express	C53F	1980	
EFO800W	Bedford YMT	Plaxton Supreme IV	C45F	1981	
A646GLD	Volvo B10M-61	Plaxton Paramount 3200	C53F	1984	Ex Capital, W Drayton, 1987
E65EVJ	Bedford CF	Steedrive Parflo	M12	1987	
E726LWP	Volvo B10M-61	Plaxton Paramount 3200 III	C53F	1988	
E559UHS	Volvo B10M-61	Plaxton Paramount 3200 III	C53F	1988	Ex Parks, Hamilton, 1990
F992HGE	Volvo B10M-61	Plaxton Paramount 3200 III	C53F	1989	Ex Parks, Hamilton, 1991

Previous Registrations:
DJS203   NNK823P

Livery: Ivory and green.

Without the fleetname, this vehicle could almost be mistaken for a Yeomans vehicle. This is not surprising since it is standing in Hereford bus station on a stand where Yeomans vehicles appear. MCJ900P was, however, new in 1976 to Miss Staples of Leominster who trades as Lugg Valley.
Phillip Stephenson

Photographed in Hereford while working service 114 to Bobblestock is Lugg Valley NUY312T, one of the shorter Bedfords, the YLQ. This example carries a Plaxton Supreme IV in which forty-five seats are provided. *David Donati*

The older vehicles in the Lugg Valley fleet feature Duple bodies, while later deliveries turned to Plaxton. These are often found on stage work in the Hereford and border areas. Formerly in the Yeoman fleet is PVJ300M, seen unloading passengers at Sutton St Nicholas while working the Hereford to Marden service in the spring of 1994. *Martin Perry*

MARTIN PERRY

Martin Parry, Bromyard Omnibus, Streamhall Garage, Linton Trading Estate, Bromyard, Hereford & Worcester, HR7 4QL

VOR814N	Bedford YRQ	Duple Dominant	C45F	1974	Ex Markham, Kingsland, 1994
JDK911P	Bristol RESL6L	East Lancashire	DP42F	1975	Ex Devon Services, Totnes, 1993
ORS86R	Leyland Leopard PSU4E/4R	Alexander AY	DP45F	1977	Ex D & G, Rachus, 1993
PUR910R	Bedford YLQ	Duple Dominant II	C45F	1977	Ex Markham, Kingsland, 1994
YSG653W	Seddon Pennine 7	Alexander AYS	B53F	1980	Ex D & G, Rachus, 1993
D186NON	Freight Rover Sherpa	Carlyle	B20F	1980	Ex Beeline, Warminster, 1994

Livery: Red and cream

Martin Perry's Bromyard Omnibus Company has long favoured Leyland service buses, though ORS86R, a former Grampian Leopard, is the sole current example. Fitted with an Alexander AY-type body it is seen here on 31st March 1994 working the Thursday-only 427 Bromyard to Martley service. *Martin Perry*

MERRY HILL MINI

Merry Hill Minibus Ltd, 100 Dudley Road East, Oldbury,
West Midlands, B69 3HG

101-138			Freight Rover Sherpa		Carlyle Citybus 2		B20F		1988		
101	E351VOJ	109	E226VOH	116	E819VOJ	124	F874XOE	133	F883XOE
102	E356VOJ	110	E514TOV	117	E820VOJ	127	F877XOE	134	F884XOE
103	E355VOJ	111	E135VOK	118	E132VOK	128	F878XOE	135	F885XOE
104	E227VOH	112	E821VOJ	119	E133VOK	129	F879XOE	136	F886XOE
105	E353VOJ	113	E134VOK	120	E818VOJ	131	F881XOE	137	F887XOE
106	E229VOH	114	E822VOJ	123	F873XOE	132	F882XOE	138	F888XOE
107	E228VOH	115	E230VOH						

139	C684WNX	Freight Rover Sherpa	Carlyle	B20F	1985	Ex Richardson, Merry Hill, 1991
140	H723LOL	Freight Rover Sherpa	Carlyle Citybus 2	B20F	1990	
141	G227EOA	Freight Rover Sherpa	Carlyle Citybus 2	B20F	1990	Ex Skills, Nottingham, 1991
142	G228EOA	Freight Rover Sherpa	Carlyle Citybus 2	B20F	1989	Ex Carlyle Hire, 1991
144	H713LOL	Freight Rover Sherpa	Carlyle Citybus 2	B20F	1990	Ex Strathclyde Buses, 1992
145	H714LOL	Freight Rover Sherpa	Carlyle Citybus 2	B20F	1990	Ex Strathclyde Buses, 1991

146-153			Freight Rover Sherpa		Carlyle Citybus 2		B20F		1989		Ex National Welsh, 1992-93
146	G273HBO	148	G264GKG	150	G267GKG	152	G271GKG	153	G272GKG
147	G263GKG	149	G265GKG	151	G270GKG				

	E200TUE	MCW MetroRider MF150/82	MCW	B25F	1988	Ex Richardson, Merry Hill, 1991
	H727LOL	Mercedes-Benz 811D	Carlyle	B33F	1990	Ex Carlyle demonstrator, 1991

Livery: Silver and black.

Merry Hill Mini was granted an operators licence for 100 vehicles in 1988, but the fleet only reached half that size at its peak, and has recently contracted a little. Throughout the period it has operated, it has run Carlyle-bodied 20-seat Freight Rovers, most of which were purchased new, not surprisingly as Carlyle had a share in the business with the owners of the Merry Hill Centre. 127, F877XOE, is probably en route to Merry Hill, but the camera has caught the dot matrix indicator in the off mode, so we cannot be certain.
Roy Marshall

MIDLAND CHOICE TRAVEL

Liyell Ltd, Watery Lane, Willenhall, West Midlands, WV13 3SU

1	TUB7M	Leyland Leopard PSU3E/4R	Plaxton Supreme III	C53F	1974	Ex Richardson, Midhurst, 1992
2	OAG175P	Leyland Leopard PSU3E/4R	Plaxton Supreme III	C53F	1976	Ex Richardson, Midhurst, 1992
3	EGB81T	Leyland National 11351A/1R		B52F	1979	Ex Western Scottish, 1992
5	ERP559T	Leyland National 11351A/1R		B49F	1979	Ex United Counties, 1992
6	SBD525R	Leyland National 11351A/1R		B49F	1979	Ex United Counties, 1992
8	PCD74R	Leyland National 11351A/1R		B49F	1976	Ex Stagecoach South, 1992
9	SFJ139R	Leyland National 11351A/1R		B52F	1977	Ex Stagecoach South, 1992
10	XLD627	Leyland TRCTL11/3RH	Plaxton Paramount 3500	C51F	1984	Ex Tayside, 1993
11	SGR131R	Leyland National 11351A/1R		B49F	1977	Ex Tees & District, 1992
12	D36KAX	Iveco Dailybus 49.10	Robin Hood City Nippy	B21F	1987	Ex Rhondda, 1992
14	PTF751L	Leyland National 1151/2R/0402		B52F	1973	Ex Ribble, 1993
15	MLG961P	Leyland National 11351/1R/SC		B49F	1975	Ex Hopkinson, Market Harborough, 1993
16	GMA409N	Leyland National 11351/1R/SC		DP48F	1974	Ex Ogden's, Haydock, 1993
17	PJI4084	Leyland National 11351/1R		B49F	1974	Ex Priory, Gosport, 1993
18	H411BVR	Mercedes-Benz 709D	Carlyle	B29F	1991	Ex Star Line, Knutsford, 1994

Previous Registrations:

XLD627	A710SSR
PJI4084	HWC83N

Livery: Green and yellow

Emerging from the shadows is PTF751L, one of the very early, dual-doored Leyland Nationals, but one given an extensive mid-life rebuilt by Ribble. The vehicle is now in the Midland Choice fleet, which as can be seen, has recently started to omit Midland from its name. *Keith Grimes*

MIDLAND RED SOUTH

Midland Red (South) Ltd, Railway Terrace, Rugby, Warwickshire, CV21 3HS
Midland Flexibus Ltd, Railway Terrace, Rugby, Warwickshire, CV21 3HS

Depots: Canal Street, Banbury; Rowley Drive, Coventry; Station Approach, Leamington Spa; Newtown Road, Nuneaton; Railway Terrace, Rugby and Avenue Farm, Stratford-on-Avon.

(A member of Stagecoach Holdings plc)

1	A75NAC	Leyland Tiger TRCTL11/2R	Plaxton Paramount 3200 E	C47FT	1983	
2	A76NAC	Leyland Tiger TRCTL11/2R	Plaxton Paramount 3200 E	C47FT	1983	
3	Q275UOC	Leyland Leopard PSU3C/4R	Plaxton P'mount 3200 E(1983)	C49F	1976	Ex Midland Red, 1981
4	230HUE	Leyland Leopard PSU3E/4R	Plaxton Supreme IV Express	C46FT	1980	Ex Midland Red North, 1981
5	331HWD	Leyland Leopard PSU3E/4R	Plaxton Supreme IV Express	C49F	1980	Ex Midland Red North, 1981
6	3273AC	Leyland Leopard PSU3E/4R	Plaxton Supreme IV Express	C46FT	1980	Ex Midland Red North, 1981
9	BVP791V	Leyland Leopard PSU3E/4R	Willowbrook 003	C49F	1980	Ex Midland Red, 1981
10	BVP801V	Leyland Leopard PSU3E/4R	Willowbrook 003	C49F	1980	Ex Midland Red, 1981
15	NPA230W	Leyland Leopard PSU3E/4R	Plaxton Supreme IV Express	C53F	1981	Ex East Midland, 1994
28	NAK28X	Leyland Leopard PSU3F/4R	Duple Dominant IV	C47F	1981	Ex East Midland, 1994

60-65

	Volvo B10M-60		Plaxton Paramount 3500 III	C48FT	1990	Ex Wallace Arnold, 1993

60	G528LWU	62	G530LWU	63	G531LWU	64	G532LWU	65	G535LWU
61	G529LWU								

Midland Red South vehicles allocated to Stratford-on-Avon were in Stratford Blue livery though Stagecoach corporate livery is now starting to appear. Plaxton Supreme Express bodywork is fitted to one of the Leyland Leopard coaches now used for local service work and 4, 230HUE, is seen waiting in Stratford about to depart for Birmingham. *Brian Pritchard*

70	BIW4977	Leyland Tiger TRCTL11/3R	Plaxton Paramount 3200 E	C49FT	1984	
73	491GAC	Leyland Tiger TRCTL11/3RH	Plaxton Paramount 3200 II	C51F	1984	
90	552OHU	Leyland Tiger TRCTL11/3R	Plaxton Paramount 3200 E	C57F	1983	Ex Cheltenham & Gloucester, 1990
91	CDG213Y	Leyland Tiger TRCTL11/3R	Plaxton Paramount 3200 E	C46FT	1983	Ex Cheltenham & Gloucester, 1991
92	420GAC	Leyland Tiger TRCTL11/3R	Plaxton Paramount 3200 E	C53F	1983	Ex Cheltenham & Gloucester, 1993
300	E433YHL	Mercedes-Benz 709D	Reeve Burgess Beaver	B25F	1988	Ex Loftys, Bridge Trafford, 1993
301	G301WHP	Mercedes-Benz 709D	PMT	B25F	1989	
302	G302WHP	Mercedes-Benz 709D	PMT	B25F	1989	
303	G303WHP	Mercedes-Benz 709D	PMT	B25F	1989	
304	J304THP	Mercedes-Benz 709D	Alexander AM	B25F	1992	
305	J305THP	Mercedes-Benz 709D	Alexander AM	B25F	1992	
306	K306ARW	Mercedes-Benz 709D	Wright	B25F	1992	
307	L307SKV	Mercedes-Benz 709D	Wright	B25F	1993	

351-360

		Ford Transit 190D	Alexander	B16F	1985	Ex Cheltenham & Gloucester, 1990

351	C616SFH	353	C620SFH	355	C623SFH	357	C625SFH	359	C646SFH
352	C619SFH	354	C622SFH	356	C624SFH	358	C628SFH	360	C647SFH

361-365

	Ford Transit 190D	Dormobile	B16F	1986	Ex East Kent, 1990/91

361	C702FKE	362	C703FKE	363	C713FKE	364	C714FKE	365	C720FKE

366-370

	Ford Transit 190D	Carlyle	B16F	1986	Ex Alder Valley, 1991

366	D313WPE	367	D314WPE	368	D315WPE	369	D320WPE	370	D321WPE

371	C729JJO	Ford Transit 190D	Carlyle	DP20F	1986	Ex Oxford Bus Company, 1991

372-382

	Ford Transit 190D	Dormobile	B16F*	1986	Ex East Kent, 1991-92
					*377/81 are DP16F

372	C708FKE	375	C722FKE	377	C707FKE	379	C710FKE	381	C717FKE
373	C718FKE	376	C706FKE	378	C709FKE	380	C711FKE	382	C719FKE
374	C721FKE								

400	F71LAL	Mercedes-Benz 811D	Alexander AM	DP33F	1989	Ex Skills, Nottingham, 1991

401-418

	Mercedes-Benz 811D	Wright	B33F*	1991	*402/4/7-12 are DP33F
					*401/3/5/6/13/7/8 are B31F

401	H401MRW	405	H495MRW	409	J409PRW	413	J413PRW	416	J416PRW
402	H402MRW	406	H406MRW	410	J410PRW	414	J414PRW	417	J417PRW
403	H403MRW	407	J407PRW	411	J411PRW	415	J415PRW	418	J418PRW
404	H404MRW	408	J408PRW	412	J412PRW				

419	G115OGA	Mercedes-Benz 811D	Alexander AM	DP33F	1988	Ex Beaton, Blantyre, 1992

420-425

	Mercedes-Benz 811D	Wright	B31F	1993

420	K420ARW	422	K422ARW	423	K423ARW	424	K424ARW	425	K425ARW
421	K421ARW								

426	F846TLU	Mercedes-Benz 811D	Optare StarRider	C29F	1989	Ex Brents Coaches, Watford, 1993
427	H912XGA	Mercedes-Benz 814D	Reeve Burgess Beaver	DP31F	1990	Ex Loftys, Bridge Trafford, 1993

457-482

	Freight Rover Sherpa	Rootes	B16F	1987

457	D457CKV	461	D461CKV	467	D467CKV	476	D476CKV	478	D478CKV
460	D460CKV	462	D462CKV						

483	D273OOJ	Freight Rover Sherpa	Carlyle	B20F	1987	Ex Carlyle demonstrator, 1988
484	D271OOJ	Freight Rover Sherpa	Carlyle	B20F	1987	Ex Carlyle demonstrator, 1988
485	D735OOG	Freight Rover Sherpa	Carlyle	B20F	1987	Ex Carlyle demonstrator, 1988
486	D736OOG	Freight Rover Sherpa	Carlyle	B20F	1987	Ex Carlyle demonstrator, 1988
487	D755JUB	Freight Rover Sherpa	Dormobile	B20F	1986	Ex Yorkshire Rider, 1990
488	D762JUB	Freight Rover Sherpa	Dormobile	B20F	1986	Ex Yorkshire Rider, 1990

Seen here in Banbury 371, C729JJO, is a Carlyle-bodied 20-seat Ford Transit. It came to Midland Red South from City of Oxford, now known as the Oxford Bus Company, in 1991. *Ken Crawley*

Eighteen Mercedes-Benz 811D with Wright bodywork were delivered in 1991. 410, J410PRW, is one of this batch seen operating Service 218 from Evesham to Stratford in June 1993. Vehicles in this batch were named; 'Sovereign' in this case. *Ken Crawley*

502-772 — Leyland National 11351A/1R — B49F* — 1976-80 — Ex Midland Red, 1981

581/2, 602-772 are fitted with DAF engines; *624, 708 are B52F;
504/90 have variable seating with central wheelchair lift.

502	JOX502P	578	NOE578R	604	NOE604R	626	PUK626R	710	TOF710S
503	JOX503P	579	NOE579R	605	NOE605R	627	PUK627R	753	XOV753T
504	JOX504P	581	NOE581R	606	NOE606R	628	PUK628R	754	XOV754T
505	JOX505P	582	NOE582R	621	PUK621R	629	PUK629R	755	XOV755T
506	JOX506P	586	NOE586R	622	PUK622R	664	SOA664S	756	XOV756T
568	NOE568R	589	NOE589R	623	PUK623R	707	TOF707S	760	XOV760T
570	NOE570R	590	NOE590R	624	PUK624R	708	TOF708S	771	BVP771V
571	NOE571R	602	NOE602R	625	PUK625R	709	TOF709S	772	BVP772V
577	NOE577R	603	NOE603R						

816	BVP816V	Leyland National 2 NL116L11/1R (DAF)	B49F	1980	Ex Midland Red, 1981
817	BVP817V	Leyland National 2 NL116L11/1R (DAF)	B49F	1980	Ex Midland Red, 1981
818	BVP818V	Leyland National 2 NL116L11/1R (DAF)	B49F	1980	Ex Midland Red, 1981

834-848 — Iveco Daily 49.10 — Robin Hood City Nippy — B19F — 1986 — Ex Rhondda, 1992-93

834	D34KAX	843	D43KAX	845	D45KAX	847	D47KAX	848	D48KAX
835	D35KAX								

851-862 — Iveco Daily 49.10 — Robin Hood City Nippy — B19F* — 1986 — *852 is B21F

851	D851CKV	854	D854CKV	857	D857CKV	859	D859CKV	861	D861CKV
852	D852CKV	855	D855CKV	858	D858CKV	860	D860CKV	862	D862CKV
853	D853CKV	856	D856CKV						

864-868 — Iveco Daily 49.10 — Robin Hood City Nippy — B19F — 1988

864	F864PAC	865	F865PAC	866	F866PAC	867	F867PAC	868	F868PAC

871	F871UAC	Iveco Daily 49.10	Robin Hood City Nippy	B25F	1989	
872	F872UAC	Iveco Daily 49.10	Robin Hood City Nippy	B25F	1989	
873	G26XBK	Iveco Daily 49.10	Phoenix	B25F	1990	Ex Loftys, Bridge Trafford, 1993

882-888 — Iveco Daily 49.10 — Robin Hood City Nippy — DP19F* — 1986 — *882/3 are DP21F

882	D882CKV	884	D884CKV	886	D886CKV	887	D887CKV	888	D888CKV
883	D883CKV	885	D885CKV						

890	E889HHP	Peugeot-Talbot Pullman	Talbot	B21F	1987	Ex Talbot demonstrator, 1988

Midland Red South have retained many of their original allocation of Leyland Nationals and while several have received new DAF engines, 505, JOX505P continues to be powered by a Leyland unit. It is seen in Banbury where normally it can be found on town services.
Keith Grimes

There are still many Leyland Nationals in the Midland Red South fleet, that came from the split of Midland Red in 1981. 623, PUK623R, illustrates the old standard livery now being replaced by the Stagecoach group corporate colours. *Colin Lloyd*

The Parade at Leamington Spa is the location for this picture of 852, D852CKV an Iveco Daily 49.10 with Robin Hood bodywork to the City Nippy design. One of twelve from the 1986 delivery it is seen heading for Stud Farm. *Keith Grimes*

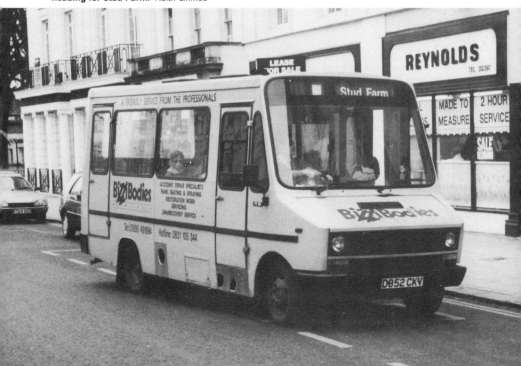

902-912   Leyland Olympian ONLXB/1R   Eastern Coach Works   H45/32F   1983-84

902	A542HAC	904	A544HAC	906	A546HAC	910	B910ODU	912	B912ODU
903	A543HAC	905	A545HAC	907	A547HAC	911	B911ODU		

939	DWF194V	Bristol VRT/SL3/6LXB	Eastern Coach Works	H43/31F	1979	Ex East Midland, 1994
940	PEU511R	Bristol VRT/SL3/6LXB	Eastern Coach Works	DPH43/31F	1977	Ex Badgerline, 1993
941	GTX746W	Bristol VRT/SL3/501	Eastern Coach Works	H43/31F	1980	Ex Red & White, 1993
943	GTX754W	Bristol VRT/SL3/501	Eastern Coach Works	H43/31F	1980	Ex Red & White, 1993
944	HUD475S	Bristol VRT/SL3/6LXB	Eastern Coach Works	H43/31F	1977	Ex Oxford Bus Company, 1993
945	HUD480S	Bristol VRT/SL3/6LXB	Eastern Coach Works	H43/31F	1977	Ex Oxford Bus Company, 1993
946	HUD479S	Bristol VRT/SL3/6LXB	Eastern Coach Works	H43/31F	1977	Ex Oxford Bus Company, 1993
947	AET181T	Bristol VRT/SL3/6LXB	Eastern Coach Works	H43/31F -	1979	Ex East Midland, 1994
948	VTV170S	Bristol VRT/SL3/6LXB	Eastern Coach Works	H43/31F	1978	Ex East Midland, 1994
949	DWF189V	Bristol VRT/SL3/6LXB	Eastern Coach Works	H43/31F	1980	Ex East Midland, 1994
952	OUC44R	Leyland Fleetline FE30AGR	MCW	H44/29F	1976	Ex Stevensons, 1989
953	OJD241R	Leyland Fleetline FE30AGR	MCW	H44/29F	1977	Ex Stevensons, 1989
954	OUC42R	Leyland Fleetline FE30AGR	MCW	H44/29F	1976	Ex Stevensons, 1990
955	OJD136R	Leyland Fleetline FE30AGR	Park Royal	H44/29F	1976	Ex Stevensons, 1990
959	YNA363M	Daimler Fleetline CRG6LXB	Northern Counties	H43/32F	1974	Ex G M Buses, 1988
960	B960ODU	Leyland Olympian ONLXB/1R	Eastern Coach Works	DPH42/30F	1984	
961	B961ODU	Leyland Olympian ONLXB/1R	Eastern Coach Works	DPH42/30F	1984	
962	C962XVC	Leyland Olympian ONLXB/1RH	Eastern Coach Works	DPH42/29F	1985	
963	C963XVC	Leyland Olympian ONLXB/1RH	Eastern Coach Works	DPH42/29F	1985	
964	C964XVC	Leyland Olympian ONLXB/1RH	Eastern Coach Works	DPH42/29F	1985	

Opposite, top: **Midland Red South** currently have the 'Easyrider' contract to provide transport for disabled persons in Coventry. Two vehicles are required, and for each service a Leyland National has been modified to allow wheelchair access at the centre door. The vehicles are painted in the West Midlands Passenger Transport 'Centro' green and yellow livery. 1051, KIB8140 was originally with London Buses. *Colin Lloyd*

Opposite, bottom: **No.953, OJD241R,** is instantly recognisable as a former London Transport DMS vehicle. It was new to London Transport in 1977, and carries the MCW version of DMS bodywork. It passed to Stevensons in 1985 and then on to Midland Red South in 1989. It was modified to single entrance layout by Stevensons. *Phillip Stephenson*

The first batch of double deckers purchased new by Midland Red South consisted of nine Leyland Olympians with Eastern Coach Works bodies. These arrived in 1983 and have been painted in different livery styles over the intervening 10 years. No.902, A542HAC, photographed in Coventry, shows the style introduced in 1992. *Colin Lloyd*

1008	KHP649N	Leyland Leopard PSU3B/4R	Duple Dominant	C53F	1975	Ex Tanners International, 1989
1009	NGU602P	Bedford YMT	Plaxton Supreme III	C53F	1976	Ex Tanners International, 1989
1010	NGU605P	Bedford YMT	Plaxton Supreme III	C53F	1976	Ex Tanners International, 1989
1015	YWK3S	Bedford YMT	Plaxton Supreme III	C53F	1978	Ex Tanners International, 1989
1017	HCS817N	Leyland Leopard PSU3/3R	Alexander AY	B53F	1975	Ex Lothian Transit, Newtongrange, 1993
1051	KIB8140	Leyland National 10351A/2R		B22DL	1978	Ex London Buses, 1991
1052	AIB4053	Leyland National 10351A/2R		B22DL	1978	Ex London Buses, 1991
1053	PIB8019	Leyland National 10351A/2R		B22DL	1977	Ex London Buses, 1991
1412	GOL412N	Leyland National 11351/1R		B49F	1975	Ex Midland Red, 1981
1553	NOE553R	Leyland National 11351A/1R		B49F	1975	Ex Midland Red, 1981
1567	NOE567R	Leyland National 11351A/1R		B49F	1975	Ex Midland Red, 1981

Previous Registrations:

230HUE	BVP786V	AIB4053	THX186S
3273AC	BVP788V	BIW4977	A70KDU
331HWD	BVP787V	F846TLU	F481FUA, REP777
420GAC	A211SAE	KHP649N	HNU123N, AIB4053
491GAC	B73OKV	KIB8140	THX249S
552OHU	A201RHT	PIB8019	THX119S
A75NAC	A190GVC, 420GAC	Q275UOC	JOX453P
A76NAC	A191GVC, 491GAC		

Livery: Stagecoach white, orange, red and blue replacing red and white.
Flexibus (green)   571, 590, 1412.

Midland Red South is a member of the Stagecoach West part of the organisation, and the first vehicles to arrive in the fleet in corporate livery were some Bristol VRTs transferred from East Midland. Now numbered 947, AET181T, it is seen in Birmingham in February 1994, still awaiting the delivery of vinyls. *Keith Grimes*

MIDLAND RED WEST

Midland Red West Ltd, Heron Lodge, London Road, Worcester,
Hereford & Worcester, WR5 2EW

Depots: Digbeth, Birmingham; Abbey Road, Evesham; Friar Street, Hereford; New Road, Kidderminster; Church Road, Redditch and Padmore Street, Worcester. Outstations are at Bishops Castle, Bridgnorth, Hopton Heath and Ludlow.

201-237

								Dennis Lance 11SDA3107		Plaxton Verde		B54F		1994	

201	L201AAB	209	L209AAB	217	L217AAB	224	L224AAB	231	L231AAB
202	L202AAB	210	L210AAB	218	L218AAB	225	L225AAB	232	L232AAB
203	L203AAB	211	L211AAB	219	L219AAB	226	L226AAB	233	L233AAB
204	L204AAB	212	L212AAB	220	L220AAB	227	L227AAB	234	L234AAB
205	L205AAB	213	L213AAB	221	L221AAB	228	L228AAB	235	L235AAB
206	L206AAB	214	L214AAB	222	L322AAB	229	L229AAB	236	L236AAB
207	L207AAB	215	L215AAB	223	L223AAB	230	L230AAB	237	L237AAB
208	L208AAB	216	L216AAB						

472	JOX472P	Leyland National 11351/1R	B49F	1975	Ex Midland Red, 1981
489	JOX489P	Leyland National 11351/1R	B49F	1975	Ex Midland Red, 1981
500	JOX500P	Leyland National 11351/1R	B49F	1976	Ex Midland Red, 1981

507-534

Leyland National 11351A/1R   B49F   1976   514 ex Midland Red East, 1982

507	JOX507P	509	JOX509P	511	JOX511P	513	JOX513P	533	JOX533P
508	JOX508P	510	JOX510P	512	JOX512P	514	JOX514P	534	JOX534P

539-550

Leyland National 11351A/1R   B49F   1976   Ex Midland Red, 1981

539	NOE539R	542	NOE542R	545	NOE545R	547	NOE547R	549	NOE549R
540	NOE540R	543	NOE543R	546	NOE546R	548	NOE548R	550	NOE550R
541	NOE541R	544	NOE544R						

585	PTT85R	Leyland National 11351A/1R	B52F	1976	Ex Devon General, 1986
600	VOD630S	Leyland National 11351A/1R	B52F	1978	Ex Western National, 1989
601	VOD601S	Leyland National 11351A/1R	B52F	1978	Ex Western National, 1989

1994 has seen the start of a major investment in Dennis Lance single deck buses for the Birmingham area where they will replace Leyland Nationals. Photographed in the first week of operation is 209, L209ABB. At that time the vehicles were mainly used on the 80s group of services to the south-west of the city.
Bill Potter

607-662 Leyland National 11351A/1R   B49F   1976-77

650 ex Midland Red East, 1983
644 ex Midland Fox, 1986; 649/53/4 ex Ribble, 1986;
617-20/34/6 ex Midland Red North, 1986, reminder ex Midland Red, 1981

607	NOE607R	618	PUK618R	634	PUK634R	650	PUK650R	658	SOA658S
608	NOE608R	620	PUK620R	636	PUK636R	653	UHG753R	660	SOA660S
609	NOE609R	630	PUK630R	644	PUK644R	654	UHG754R	661	SOA661S
610	NOE610R	632	PUK632R	646	PUK646R	656	PUK656R	662	SOA662S
617	PUK617R	633	PUK633R	649	UHG749R	657	SOA657S		

665	RDA665R	Leyland Leopard PSU3E/4R	Plaxton Supreme III Express C49F	1977	Ex Midland Red, 1981
666	RDA666R	Leyland Leopard PSU3E/4R	Plaxton Supreme III Express C49F	1977	Ex Midland Red, 1981
667	RDA667R	Leyland Leopard PSU3E/4R	Plaxton Supreme III Express C49F	1977	Ex Midland Red, 1981

711-724 Leyland National 11351A/1R   B49F   1978

711-4 ex Midland Fox, 1986
remainder ex Midland Red, 1981

711	TOF711S	714	TOF714S	721	WOC721T	723	WOC723T	724	WOC724T
712	TOF712S	720	WOC720T	722	WOC722T				

742-752 Leyland National 11351A/1R   B49F   1979   Ex Midland Red, 1981

742	XOV742T	744	XOV744T	746	XOV746T	748	XOV748T	750	XOV750T
743	XOV743T	745	XOV745T	747	XOV747T	749	XOV749T	752	XOV752T

754	AFJ754T	Leyland National 11351A/1R	B50F	1979	Ex Western National, 1990
755	AFJ755T	Leyland National 11351A/1R	B50F	1979	Ex Western National, 1989
756	AFJ756T	Leyland National 11351A/1R	B50F	1979	Ex Western National, 1990

757-773 Leyland National 11351A/1R   B49F   1979-80

757-9 ex Midland Red North, 1986
remainder ex Midland Red, 1981

757	XOV757T	759	XOV759T	762	BVP762V	770	BVP770V	773	BVP773V
758	XOV758T	761	BVP761V						

The picturesque town of Evesham is situated not only in the beautiful Vale of Evesham but on the frontier between two of the rapidly-growing groups of Badgerline and Stagecoach. Representing the former 657, SOA657S, is one of a batch of Leyland Nationals, many brought in from elsewhere.
Ken Crawley

The Birmingham to Hereford service is the remaining leg of a route that once started as far east as Leicester in BBMO days. A sunny day in Hereford sees 775, BVP775V, heading north. Many of the express service vehicles still carry Midlands Express livery. *David Donati*

| **774-783** | | Leyland Leopard PSU3E/4R | Plaxton Supreme IV | C49F* | 1979/80 | Ex Midland Red Coaches, 1986 *774/5/7 are C53F |

| 774 | BVP774V | 776 | BVP776V | 778 | BVP778V | 782 | BVP782V | 783 | BVP783V |
| 775 | BVP775V | 777 | BVP777V | 781 | BVP781V | | | | |

849	ROG549Y	Leyland Leopard PSU3A/4R	Eastern Coach Works (1983) C49F	1970	Ex Midland Red Coaches, 1986
851	ROG551Y	Leyland Leopard PSU3A/4R	Eastern Coach Works (1983) C49F	1970	Ex Midland Red Coaches, 1986
852	ROG552Y	Leyland Leopard PSU3A/4R	Eastern Coach Works (1983) C49F	1970	Ex Midland Red Coaches, 1986
853	Q553UOC	Leyland Leopard PSU3F/4R	Plaxton P'mount 3200 (1984) C34FT	1982	Ex Midland Red Coaches, 1986
854	Q276UOC	Leyland Leopard PSU3E/4R	Plaxton P'mount 3200 (1983) C49F	1980	Ex Midland Red, 1981
1001	FEH1Y	Leyland Tiger TRCTL11/3R	Plaxton Paramount 3500	C50FT	1983	

| **1002-1007** | | Leyland Tiger TRCTL11/3RH | Plaxton Paramount 3200 II | C50FT* | 1985 | *1006/7 are C39FT |

| 1002 | B102JAB | 1004 | B104JAB | 1005 | B105JAB | 1006 | B106JAB | 1007 | B107JAB |
| 1003 | B103JAB | | | | | | | | |

1008	LOA832X	Leyland Tiger TRCTL11/3R	Plaxton Supreme IV	C51F	1981	Ex Midland Red Coaches, 1986
1010	EAH890Y	Leyland Tiger TRCTL11/3R	Plaxton Paramount 3200 E	C53F	1983	Ex Midland Red Coaches, 1986
1011	A895KCL	Leyland Tiger TRCTL11/3R	Plaxton Paramount 3200 E	C53F	1983	Ex Midland Red Coaches, 1986
1012	A896KCL	Leyland Tiger TRCTL11/3R	Plaxton Paramount 3200 E	C53F	1983	Ex Midland Red Coaches, 1986
1013	A678KDV	Leyland Tiger TRCTL11/3R	Plaxton Paramount 3500	C48FT	1983	Ex Midland Red Coaches, 1986
1014	A656VDA	Leyland Tiger TRCTL11/3R	Plaxton Paramount 3500	C48FT	1983	Ex Midland Red Coaches, 1986
1015	A657VDA	Leyland Tiger TRCTL11/3R	Plaxton Paramount 3500	C48FT	1983	Ex Midland Red Coaches, 1986
1016	A658VDA	Leyland Tiger TRCTL11/3R	Plaxton Paramount 3200	C50F	1983	Ex Midland Red Coaches, 1986
1017	B566BOK	Leyland Tiger TRCTL11/3RH	Duple Caribbean 2	C48FT	1984	Ex Midland Red Coaches, 1986
1018	B567BOK	Leyland Tiger TRCTL11/3RH	Duple Caribbean 2	C48FT	1984	Ex Midland Red Coaches, 1986
1019	B568BOK	Leyland Tiger TRCTL11/3RH	Duple Caribbean 2	C48FT	1984	Ex Midland Red Coaches, 1986
1020	C985HOX	Leyland Tiger TRCTL11/3RZ	Duple 340	C49FT	1986	Ex Midland Red Coaches, 1986
1021	C986HOX	Leyland Tiger TRCTL11/3RZ	Duple 340	C49FT	1986	Ex Midland Red Coaches, 1986
1022	C987HOX	Leyland Tiger TRCTL11/3RZ	Duple 340	C49FT	1986	Ex Midland Red Coaches, 1986

1101-1150   Leyland Lynx LX2R11C15Z4R   Leyland Lynx   B49F   1990

1101	G101HNP	1111	G111HNP	1121	G121HNP	1131	G131HNP	1141	G141HNP
1102	G102HNP	1112	G112HNP	1122	G122HNP	1132	G132HNP	1142	G142HNP
1103	G103HNP	1113	G113HNP	1123	G123HNP	1133	G133HNP	1143	G143HNP
1104	G104HNP	1114	G114HNP	1124	G124HNP	1134	G134HNP	1144	G144HNP
1105	G105HNP	1115	G115HNP	1125	G125HNP	1135	G135HNP	1145	G145HNP
1106	G106HNP	1116	G116HNP	1126	G126HNP	1136	G136HNP	1146	G146HNP
1107	G107HNP	1117	G117HNP	1127	G127HNP	1137	G137HNP	1147	G147HNP
1108	G108HNP	1118	G118HNP	1128	G128HNP	1138	G138HNP	1148	G148HNP
1109	G109HNP	1119	G119HNP	1129	G129HNP	1139	G139HNP	1149	G149HNP
1110	G110HNP	1120	G120HNP	1130	G130HNP	1140	G140HNP	1150	G150HNP

1300	A670XUK	Mercedes-Benz L307D	Devon Conversions	C12F	1984	Ex Midland Red Coaches, 1986

1301-1319   Mercedes-Benz L608D   PMT Hanbridge   B20F*   1985   *1301-6 are DP20F

1301	C301PNP	1305	C305PNP	1309	C309PNP	1313	C313PNP	1317	C317PNP
1302	C302PNP	1306	C306PNP	1310	C310PNP	1314	C314PNP	1318	C318PNP
1303	C303PNP	1307	C307PNP	1311	C311PNP	1315	C315PNP	1319	C319PNP
1304	C304PNP	1308	C308PNP	1312	C312PNP	1316	C316PNP		

1320	C320PNP	Mercedes-Benz L608D	Alexander	B20F	1986

1321-1361   Mercedes-Benz L608D   Robin Hood   B20F   1985-86

1321	C321PNP	1330	C330PNP	1338	C338PNP	1346	C346PNP	1354	C354PNP
1322	C322PNP	1331	C331PNP	1339	C339PNP	1347	C347PNP	1355	C355PNP
1323	C323PNP	1332	C332PNP	1340	C340PNP	1348	C348PNP	1356	C356PNP
1324	C324PNP	1333	C333PNP	1341	C341PNP	1349	C349PNP	1357	C357PNP
1325	C325PNP	1334	C334PNP	1342	C342PNP	1350	C350PNP	1358	C358PNP
1326	C326PNP	1335	C335PNP	1343	C343PNP	1351	C351PNP	1359	C359PNP
1327	C327PNP	1336	C336PNP	1344	C344PNP	1352	C352PNP	1360	C360PNP
1328	C328PNP	1337	C337PNP	1345	C345PNP	1353	C353PNP	1361	C361RUY
1329	C329PNP								

1362-1384   Mercedes-Benz L608D   Reeve Burgess   B20F   1986

1362	C362RUY	1367	C367RUY	1372	C372RUY	1377	C377RUY	1381	C381RUY
1363	C363RUY	1368	C368RUY	1373	C373RUY	1378	C378RUY	1382	C382RUY
1364	C364RUY	1369	C369RUY	1374	C374RUY	1379	C379RUY	1383	C383RUY
1365	C365RUY	1370	C370RUY	1375	C375RUY	1380	C380RUY	1384	C384RUY
1366	C366RUY	1371	C371RUY	1376	C376RUY				

1385-1404   Mercedes-Benz L608D   Robin Hood   B20F   1986

1385	C385RUY	1389	C389RUY	1393	C393RUY	1397	C397RUY	1401	C401RUY
1386	C386RUY	1390	C390RUY	1394	C394RUY	1398	C398RUY	1402	C402RUY
1387	C387RUY	1391	C391RUY	1395	C395RUY	1399	C399RUY	1403	C403RUY
1388	C388RUY	1392	C392RUY	1396	C396RUY	1400	C400RUY	1404	C404RUY

1405	A669XDA	Mercedes-Benz L508D	Reeve Burgess	DP17F	1984	Ex Midland Red Coaches, 1986

1406-1439   Mercedes-Benz 609D   Reeve Burgess   B20F   1987-88

1406	E406HAB	1413	E413KUY	1420	E420KUY	1427	E427KUY	1434	E434KUY
1407	E407HAB	1414	E414KUY	1421	E421KUY	1428	E428KUY	1435	E435KUY
1408	E408HAB	1415	E415KUY	1422	E422KUY	1429	E429KUY	1436	E436KUY
1409	E409HAB	1416	E416KUY	1423	E423KUY	1430	E430KUY	1437	E437KUY
1410	E410HAB	1417	E417KUY	1424	E424KUY	1431	E431KUY	1438	E438KUY
1411	E411HAB	1418	E418KUY	1425	E425KUY	1432	E432KUY	1439	E439KUY
1412	E412KUY	1419	E419KUY	1426	E426KUY	1433	E433KUY		

Opposite, top: **At the height of the minibus boom in the 1980s Walter Alexander of Falkirk filled part of the large NBC order book converting vans to feed the seemingly insatiable demand. Some time later a coach built version on chassis-cowls was introduced, coded AM. An example of the earlier van-conversion is 1455, C212PCD, initially allocated to NBC company Southdown.** *Phillip Stephenson*

Opposite, bottom: **The Plaxton Verde has been chosen for the 1994 vehicle requirement and thirty-seven buses are being delivered to Midland Red West where they will replace many of the older Leyland Nationals. An early arrival is 210, L210ABB, seen in the Northfield area of the city.** *Bill Potter*

1440	C475BHY	Mercedes-Benz L608D		Reeve Burgess		B20F	1986	Ex Bristol Omnibus, 1988	

1441-1449		Mercedes-Benz L608D		Reeve Burgess		B20F	1986	Ex Southdown, 1988	
1441	C581SHC	**1443**	C583SHC	**1445**	C585SHC	**1447**	C587SHC	**1449**	C589SHC
1442	C582SHC	**1444**	C584SHC	**1446**	C586SHC	**1448**	C588SHC		

1450	C788FRL	Mercedes-Benz L608D	Reeve Burgess	B20F	1986	Ex Western National, 1989
1451	C790FRL	Mercedes-Benz L608D	Reeve Burgess	B20F	1986	Ex Western National, 1989
1452	C207PCD	Mercedes-Benz L608D	Alexander	B20F	1986	Ex Brighton & Hove, 1990
1453	C208PCD	Mercedes-Benz L608D	Alexander	B20F	1986	Ex Brighton & Hove, 1990
1454	C209PCD	Mercedes-Benz L608D	Alexander	B20F	1986	Ex Brighton & Hove, 1990
1455	C212PCD	Mercedes-Benz L608D	Alexander	B20F	1986	Ex Brighton & Hove, 1990

1476-1499		Mercedes-Benz L608D		Reeve Burgess		B20F	1986	Ex City Line, 1993	
1476	C476BHY	**1487**	C487BHY	**1490**	C490BHY	**1492**	C492BHY	**1498**	C498BHY
1477	C477BHY	**1488**	C488BHY	**1491**	C491BHY	**1497**	C497BHY	**1499**	C499BHY
1483	C483BHY								

1801-1808		Peugeot-Talbot Pullman		Talbot		B22F	1990		
1801	H201JHP	**1803**	H203JHP	**1806**	H206JHP	**1807**	H207JHP	**1808**	H208JHP
1802	H202JHP	**1804**	H204JHP						

Previous Registrations:

ROG549Y	WHA249H	ROG552Y	WHA255H	Q553UOC	LOA843X
ROG551Y	WHA254H	Q276UOC	BVP804V		

Livery: Red, cream and black;
yellow and green   (Quickstep: 1801-8)

Badgerline's first major investment in the Midland Red West subsidiary was a batch of fifty Leyland Lynx introduced in 1990. Photographed outside the Church of St Stephen is 1145, G145HNP represents this multi-million pound commitment to fleet renewal. *Bill Potter*

Left: **Quickstep** is a West Midlands PTE (Centro) marketing name for some of its tendered services. To operate those to which it is contracted, Midland Red West have a batch of Peugeot-Talbot Pullmans. The low floor layout makes these vehicles attractive to the less-able passenger. *Tony Wilson*

One of the early Leyland Nationals brought from the original Midland Red company is TOF712S, photographed in Redditch. *Ken Jubb*

NEWBURY COACHES

KR, KM & AR Powell, Lower Road Trading Estate, Ledbury, Hereford & Worcester, HR8 2DJ

XVJ155T	Bedford YMT	Plaxton Supreme IV Express	C53F	1979	
DWK407T	Bedford YMT	Plaxton Supreme IV	C53F	1979	Ex Bryant, Williton, 1994
DVJ398W	Bedford YMT	Plaxton Supreme IV Express	C53F	1980	
MDG193W	Bedford YMT (Cummins)	Plaxton Supreme IV Express	C53F	1980	Ex Berline, Gloucester, 1984
C402XFO	Bedford YNV Venturer	Plaxton Paramount 3200 II	C57F	1986	
C355ALJ	Bedford YNV Venturer	Plaxton Paramount 3200 II	C57F	1986	Ex Brixham Coaches, 1989
D95ALR	Bedford YMP	Plaxton Paramount 3200 II	C41F	1986	Ex Quo-Vadis, Longford, 1993
D439BCJ	Bedford YNV Venturer	Plaxton Paramount 3200 III	C52FT	1987	
E830EUT	Bedford YNV Venturer	Plaxton Paramount 3200 III	C57F	1988	Ex Wainfleet, Nuneaton, 1990
E833EUT	Bedford YNV Venturer	Plaxton Paramount 3200 III	C57F	1988	Ex Wainfleet, Nuneaton, 1991
F803KCJ	Dennis Javelin 12SDA1907	Plaxton Paramount 3200 III	C57F	1988	
F784KVJ	Ford Transit VE6	Crystals	M16	1988	
F944MCJ	Ford Transit VE6	Crystals	M16	1989	
J663CVJ	Leyland Tiger TRCTL11/3AR	Plaxton Paramount 3200 III	C57F	1992	
K830HVJ	Renault Master T35D	Pearl	M16	1993	

Livery: White and blue

Ledbury is one of the attractive towns in Herefordshire noted for the old market area. Used as a waiting area for the bus services, it forms the background to this recent photograph of Newbury Coaches' XVJ155T, The name of the operation comes from the cottages in the town from where the business began. *Bill Potter*

NORTH BIRMINGHAM BUSWAYS

North Birmingham Busways Ltd, 5 Alwyn Walk, Birmingham, West Midlands, B23 7YY

Depot: Eastwoods, 84 Wood Lane, Erdington.

JFV317S	Leyland Atlantean AN68A/2R	East Lancashire	H50/36F	1978	Ex Blackpool, 1994
JFV318S	Leyland Atlantean AN68A/2R	East Lancashire	H50/36F	1978	Ex Blackpool, 1994
JFV319S	Leyland Atlantean AN68A/2R	East Lancashire	H50/36F	1978	Ex Blackpool, 1994
JFV320S	Leyland Atlantean AN68A/2R	East Lancashire	H50/36F	1978	Ex Blackpool, 1994
URN321V	Leyland Atlantean AN68A/2R	East Lancashire	H50/36F	1979	Ex Blackpool, 1994

Livery: Cream and green

North Birmingham Busways have commenced operations to the north of the city with five Leyland Atlanteans, all with East Lancashire bodywork and previously with Blackpool Transport. The livey chosen is based on the Blackpool scheme, though the lower panels have been repainted before the application of new fleet names. Photographed in Birmingham Road, Sutton, is URN321V, the newest of the quintet. *D E Wall*

City of Oxford have been operating the Oxford to London service using batches of Duple-bodied Leyland Leopards for many years and, although the combination was changed some ten years ago, several of these survive on other 'CityLink' services. One of the four longest serving examples is 24, BBW24V. *Colin Lloyd*

The recent choice for the high-frequency, premier service from Oxford to the capital is the Dennis Javelin with Plaxton Premiére bodywork. First of a batch of six received in 1992 is 50, K750UJO. *Colin Lloyd*

OXFORD BUS COMPANY
WYCOMBE BUS COMPANY

City of Oxford Motor Services Ltd, 395 Cowley Road, Oxford, Oxfordshire, OX4 2DJ

A member of Go-Ahead Group Ltd.
Depots: Cowley Road, Oxford and Newlands Road, High Wycombe

20	BBW20V	Leyland Leopard PSU3E/4R	Duple Dominant II Express	C49F	1979	
21	BBW21V	Leyland Leopard PSU3E/4R	Duple Dominant II Express	C49F	1979	
23	BBW23V	Leyland Leopard PSU3E/4R	Duple Dominant II Express	C49F	1979	
24	BBW24V	Leyland Leopard PSU3E/4R	Duple Dominant II Express	C49F	1979	

50-55
Dennis Javelin 12SDA2118 · Plaxton Premiére 320 · C53F · 1992

| 50 | K750UJO | 52 | K752UJO | 53 | K753UJO | 54 | K754UJO | 55 | K755UJO |
| 51 | K751UJO | | | | | | | | |

100	YPJ209Y	Leyland Tiger TRCTL11/3R	Plaxton Paramount 3500	C50F	1983	Ex The Bee Line, 1990
105	EBW105Y	Leyland Tiger TRCTL11/3R	Duple Dominant IV Express	C50F	1983	
107	EBW107Y	Leyland Tiger TRCTL11/3R	Duple Dominant IV Express	C50F	1983	
108	EBW108Y	Leyland Tiger TRCTL11/3R	Duple Dominant IV Express	C50F	1983	
111	A111MUD	Leyland Tiger TRCTL11/3RH	Plaxton Paramount 3200 E	C51F	1984	
112	A112MUD	Leyland Tiger TRCTL11/3RH	Plaxton Paramount 3200 E	C51F	1984	
113	A113MUD	Leyland Tiger TRCTL11/3RH	Plaxton Paramount 3200 E	C51F	1984	
114	A114MUD	Leyland Tiger TRCTL11/3RH	Plaxton Paramount 3200 E	C51F	1984	

115-119
Leyland Tiger TRCTL11/3RH · Plaxton Paramount 3500 E · C50F · 1984

| 115 | A115PBW | 116 | A116PBW | 117 | A117PBW | 118 | A118PBW | 119 | A119PBW |

120-124
Leyland Tiger TRCTL11/3RH · Plaxton Paramount 3500 IIE · C51F · 1984

| 120 | B120UUD | 121 | B121UUD | 122 | B122UUD | 123 | B123UUD | 124 | B124UUD |

130-134
DAF MB230LT615 · Plaxton Paramount 3500 III · C53F · 1988

| 130 | E130YUD | 131 | E131YUD | 132 | E132YUD | 133 | E133YUD | 134 | E134YUD |

The final batch of Leyland Leopards with Duple Dominant bodies delivered for CityLink work were EBW-Ys of 1983. Now supporting a modified front grill resembling that from a Plaxton Paramount is 106, EBW106Y.
Colin Lloyd

Six Leyland Olympians built at Lillyhall formed the double-deck requirement for 1990, and followed five earlier examples in having dual-doored bodywork from Alexander's Falkirk plant. Oxford Bus Company 232, G232VWL, is seen unusually working a CityLink 190 duty passing the Central Music Library on its way to Victoria Coach Station. *Colin Lloyd*

Representing the final batch of Eastern Coach Works-bodied Leyland Olympians to enter the Oxford Bus Company fleet is 205, VJO205X. Now approaching 12 years old this batch should look over its metaphorical shoulders as VRTs delivered the previous year are currently being withdrawn. *Malc MacDonald.*

135-139	DAF SB3000DKV601	Plaxton Paramount 3500 III	C53F	1989		
135 F135LJO	**136** F136LJO	**137** F137LJO	**138** F138LJO	**139** F139LJO		

140	J140NJO	DAF SB2305DHS585	Plaxton Paramount 3200 III	C53F	1991
141	J141NJO	DAF SB2305DHS585	Plaxton Paramount 3200 III	C53F	1991

150-155	Volvo B10M-62	Plaxton Premiére 350	C53F	1994		
150 L150HUD	**152** L152HUD	**153** L153HUD	**154** L154HUD	**155** L155HUD		
151 L151HUD						

201-224	Leyland Olympian ONLXB/1R*	Eastern Coach Works	H47/28D	1982-83	*221 is ONLXC/1R

201 VJO201X	**206** VJO206X	**211** WWL211X	**216** BBW216Y	**221** CUD221Y
202 VJO202X	**207** WWL207X	**212** WWL212X	**217** BBW217Y	**222** CUD222Y
203 VJO203X	**208** WWL208X	**213** BBW213Y	**218** BBW218Y	**223** CUD223Y
204 VJO204X	**209** WWL209X	**214** BBW214Y	**219** CUD219Y	**224** CUD224Y
205 VJO205X	**210** WWL210X	**215** BBW215Y	**220** CUD220Y	

225-229	Leyland Olympian ONLXB/1RH	Alexander RL	H47/26D	1988	
225 E225CFC	**226** E226CFC	**227** E227CFC	**228** E228CFC	**229** E229CFC

230-235	Leyland Olympian ON2R50G16Z4	Alexander RL	H47/26D	1990	
230 G230VWL	**232** G232VWL	**233** G233VWL	**234** G234VWL	**235** G235VWL
231 G231VWL				

236	FWL778Y	Leyland Olympian ONLXB/1R	Eastern Coach Works	H45/32F	1983	Ex UKAEA, Harwell, 1991
237	FWL779Y	Leyland Olympian ONLXB/1R	Eastern Coach Works	H45/32F	1983	Ex UKAEA, Harwell, 1991
238	FWL780Y	Leyland Olympian ONLXB/1R	Eastern Coach Works	H45/32F	1983	Ex UKAEA, Harwell, 1991
239	FWL781Y	Leyland Olympian ONLXB/1R	Eastern Coach Works	H45/32F	1983	Ex UKAEA, Harwell, 1991

The 1994 delivery of new coaching stock includes 151, L151HUD, one of a batch of six Volvo B10M-62s. This new designation indicated the mark IV version of this highly-popular B10M chassis and its small increase in wheelbase length. Plaxton Premiére 350 bodywork is carried, demonstrated as it arrives at Heathrow in February of this year. *Colin Lloyd*

474-515			Bristol VRT/SL3/6LXB		Eastern Coach Works	H43/27D	1978-81		
474	HUD474S	478	HUD478S	486	OUD486T	500	HUD500W	507	KJO507W
476	HUD476S	481	HUD481S	494	HUD494W	505	KJO505W	512	PFC512W
477	HUD477S	484	OUD484T	499	HUD499W				

611	RFC11T	Leyland Leopard PSU3E/4R	Willowbrook Warrior (1991)	B48F	1978	
612	WPD27Y	Leyland Leopard PSU3G/4R	Willowbrook Warrior (1991)	B48F	1982	Ex The Bee Line, 1990
613	RFC13T	Leyland Leopard PSU3E/4R	Willowbrook Warrior (1991)	B48F	1978	
614	RFC14T	Leyland Leopard PSU3E/4R	Willowbrook Warrior (1991)	B48F	1978	
627	MUD27W	Leyland Leopard PSU3F/4R	Willowbrook Warrior (1990)	B48F	1981	
631	VUD31X	Leyland Leopard PSU3G/4R	Willowbrook Warrior (1991)	B48F	1982	
633	VUD33X	Leyland Leopard PSU3G/4R	Willowbrook Warrior (1990)	B48F	1982	

750-762			MCW MetroRider MF150/26*		MCW		B25F	1987	*750 is MF150/13
									*758-62 are MF150/51
750	D750SJO	753	E753VJO	756	E756VJO	759	E759XWL	761	E761XWL
751	E751VJO	754	E754VJO	757	E757VJO	760	E760XWL	762	E762XWL
752	E752VJO	755	E755VJO	758	E758XWL				

763	F763LBW	MCW MetroRider MF150/114	MCW	B25F	1989

764-768			MCW MetroRider MF150/109*		MCW		B23F	1989	Ex Merthyr Tydfil, 1989
									*768 is MF150/105
764	F501ANY	765	F502ANY	766	F503ANY	767	F504ANY	768	F505CBO

769-783			Optare MetroRider MR09		Optare		B25F	1990	
769	G769WFC	772	G772WFC	775	G775WFC	778	G778WFC	781	G781WFC
770	G770WFC	773	G773WFC	776	G776WFC	779	G779WFC	782	G782WFC
771	G771WFC	774	G774WFC	777	G777WFC	780	G780WFC	783	G783WFC

Oxford are unique amongst former NBC subsidiaries for two notable reasons. Firstly, as is often quoted, they were the only stage carriage fleet not to receive Leyland Nationals (that is until they took over the High Wycombe operations of The Bee Line) and they are the only subsidiary to purchase Willowbrook Warrior re-bodies. These were fitted to six former CityLink Leopard chassis and one from The Bee Line fleet. No.633, VUD33X, is seen in Oxford. *Keith Grimes*

Oxford's traffic problems have prompted another experiment with battery operated buses. In a joint venture between Southern Electric, Oxfordshire County Council and Oxford Bus Company four electric-powered Optare MetroRiders were introduced in 1993. The lower seating capacity is a result of the weight penalty imposed by the storage of the batteries. No.802, L802HJO awaits time outside the rail station. *Phillip Stephenson*

801	L801HJO	Optare MetroRider MR??	Optare	B18F	1993	On loan from Southern Electric	
802	L802HJO	Optare MetroRider MR??	Optare	B18F	1993	On loan from Southern Electric	
803	L803HJO	Optare MetroRider MR??	Optare	B18F	1993	On loan from Southern Electric	
804	L804HJO	Optare MetroRider MR??	Optare	B18F	1993	On loan from Southern Electric	

950-975

		Leyland Titan TNLXB2RRSp	Leyland		H44/26D*	1981-83	Ex London Buses, 1993 *957-60 are H44/24D

950	GYE280W	956	KYV519X	961	KYV524X	966	KYV381X	971	KYV457X
951	KYV516X	957	KYN291X	962	KYV530X	967	KYV392X	972	
952	KYV300W	958	KYV370X	963	OHV727Y	968	NUW661Y	973	
953	KYV317X	959	NUW667Y	964	OHV745Y	969	KYV510X	974	NUW635Y
954	KYV328X	960	OHV711Y	965	OHV783Y	970	KYN308X	975	A869SUL
955	KYV452X								

999	PWL999W	Leyland Olympian B45/TL11/2R	Alexander RL	H50/34D	1980	Ex Leyland demonstrator, 1987
1103	EBW103Y	Leyland Tiger TRCTL11/3R	Duple Dominant IV Express	C51F	1983	
1104	EBW104Y	Leyland Tiger TRCTL11/3R	Duple Dominant IV Express	C51F	1983	
1106	EBW106Y	Leyland Tiger TRCTL11/3R	Duple Dominant IV Express	C51F	1983	
1109	EBW109Y	Leyland Tiger TRCTL11/3R	Duple Dominant IV Express	C50F	1983	
1110	EBW110Y	Leyland Tiger TRCTL11/3R	Duple Dominant IV Express	C50F	1983	

1321-1353

		Leyland National 11351/1R		B49F	1974-75 Ex The Bee Line, 1990

1321	TBL165M	1344	KPA357P	1346	KPA359P	1351	KPA377P	1353	KPA384P
1328	TBL172M								

Five Leyland Lynx were added to The Bee Line fleet during 1988, all being placed in service at High Wycombe. These duly passed to Oxford who continue to use them at Wycombe. In the latest livery is 1403, F558NJM, seen in the town. *Colin Lloyd*

Opposite top: The acquisition of the former London Buses Leyland Titans was continuing as this book went to press by which time some twenty-four examples were in service. One of the more recent arrivals was 969, KYV501X seen here in Worcester Street, Oxford in February 1994. *Colin Lloyd*

Opposite bottom: Oxford Bus Company's minibus livery employs Oxford City Nipper branding as demonstrated by 758, E758XWL. All 38 MetroRiders wear this scheme except for the four City Circuit Electric buses. *Bill Potter*

The arrival of Leyland Nationals into the Oxford fleet has already been commented upon earlier. Wearing the titles for the Wycombe fleet is 1353, KPA384P, is seen heading for Micklefield, a housing area to the east of the town. *Colin Lloyd*

1354	KPA390P	Leyland National 11351A/1R				B49F	1976	Ex The Bee Line, 1990	
1356	NPJ481R	Leyland National 11351A/1R				B49F	1977	Ex The Bee Line, 1990	
1360	TPE158S	Leyland National 11351A/1R				B49F	1978	Ex The Bee Line, 1990	
1377	THX177S	Leyland National 10351A/2R				DP49F	1978	Ex London Buses, 1993	
1384	VPF296S	Leyland National 11351A/1R				B45F	1978	Ex The Bee Line, 1990	

1401-1405

		Leyland Lynx LX112L10ZR1S	Leyland Lynx			B49F	1988	Ex The Bee Line, 1990	
1401	F556NJM	1402	F557NJM	1403	F558NJM	1404	F559NJM	1405	F560NJM

1508	MRJ8W	Bristol VRT/SL3/6LXB	Eastern Coach Works	DPH41/29F	1980	Ex Mayne, Manchester, 1991	
1509	MRJ9W	Bristol VRT/SL3/6LXB	Eastern Coach Works	DPH41/29F	1980	Ex Mayne, Manchester, 1991	

1543-1555

		Bristol VRT/SL3/6LXB		Eastern Coach Works		H43/31F	1976	Ex The Bee Line, 1990	
1543	GGM110W	1546	HJB453W	1549	HJB456W	1552	HJB459W	1554	HJB461W
1544	HJB451W	1547	HJB454W	1550	HJB457W	1553	HJB460W	1555	HJB462W
1545	HJB452W	1548	HJB455W	1551	HJB458W				

1563	CJH124V	Bristol VRT/SL3/6LXB	Eastern Coach Works	DPH43/31F	1980	Ex The Bee Line, 1990	
1726	MUD26W	Leyland Leopard PSU3F/4R	Duple Dominant IV Express	C49F	1981		
1763	A213DPB	Leyland Tiger TRCTL11/3RH	Plaxton Paramount 3200 E	C51F	1983	Ex The Bee Line, 1990	
1822	D822UTF	Leyland Olympian ONLXB/1RH	Eastern Coach Works	CH39/21F	1986	Ex The Bee Line, 1990	
1823	D823UTF	Leyland Olympian ONLXB/1RH	Eastern Coach Works	CH39/21F	1986	Ex The Bee Line, 1990	
1824	D824UTF	Leyland Olympian ONLXB/1RH	Eastern Coach Works	CH39/21F	1986	Ex The Bee Line, 1990	

Liveries: Red, white and black (buses); Blue, yellow and white (City Link coaches).
Park & Ride: 225-9, 954/8, 999

Operating units:
Wycombe Bus Company: 23/4, 1104/6/9/10, 1321/8/44/51/3/4/6/60/77/84, 1401-5, 1508/9/43-52/4/5/63, 1726/63, 1822-4.
Oxford Bus Company: Remainder.

Ordered by Southern Vectis, but diverted to Berks Bucks Bus Co because of the privatisation of the former, this final double-deck coach design from Eastern Coach Works was based on the Leyland Olympian . The three examples carry this unique style which was aimed at attracting the NBC orders away from MCW and the Metroliner design. Photographed leaving High Wycombe for Aylesbury is 1824, D824UTF. *Colin Lloyd*

Oxford Bus Company have taken into stock around twenty-six Leyland Titans formerly working with London Buses. Though a few entered service in London Buses livery, many have now been painted into full livery and 960 is seen looking very smart as it passes the new Thames Transit Darts on its way to Blackbird Leys. *Bill Potter*

In addition to the Leyland Nationals from The Bee Line, Oxford have taken another National, this time one with high-back seating from the London Buses fleet. Photographed in Reading is 1377, THX177S.
Phillip Stephenson

One of a dwindling number of Bristol VRTs remaining with Oxford is 476, HUD476S, retaining the 'traditional' duck-egg blue livery. The vehicle is seen on the service to Blackbird Leys, the destination now receiving competition from Thames Transit. It is seen in the City on a recent sunny February morning.
Keith Grimes

Storm-clouds gather over the Park & Ride car-park at Pear Tree Hill, north Oxford, as newly-painted Leyland Titan 958, KYV370X awaits passengers. One of three of Oxford Bus Company's Titans to be in a white livery (the third being an overall advert), it sports the Park & Ride lettering on the roof coveing. The dark clouds that form the background contrast with the white scheme. *Bill Potter*

One of the original batch of five Alder Valley grant-coaches, and only one of two coaches allocated to High Wycombe. Purchased in October 1993 for express services, the batch has now been scattered. Seen at Wembly while on private hire work is 1763, A213DPB. *Colin Lloyd*

OXON TRAVEL

A Sidhu & M S Purewal, The Old Vicarage, Cavers Field, Bicester, Oxfordshire, OX6 9TH

Depot: Station Approach, London Road, Bicester.

KJD431P	Bristol LH6L	Eastern Coach Works	B39F	1976	Ex Routemaster Travel, Aylesbury, 1994
OJD17R	Bristol LHS6L	Eastern Coach Works	B26F	1976	Ex Devon Services, Paignton, 1994
ATH108T	Bristol LHS6L	Plaxton Supreme III	DP35F	1979	Ex Castle Garage, Llandovery, 1994
APM118T	AEC Reliance 6U2R	Plaxton Supreme IV Express	C49F	1979	Ex Routemaster Travel, Aylesbury, 1994

Previous Registrations:
ATH108T   FTW133T, 100OX

Livery: Red

A recent entrant into stage-carriage work in Oxfordshire, Oxon Travel were running into Bicester half-hourly as this Bus Handbook was prepared. The route is operated with two Bristol LHSs and this LH, KJD431P, one of many supplied to London Buses in 1976. *Keith Grimes*

PATTERSON

D F & P M Patterson, Unit 36, Elliott Road, Selly Oak, Birmingham, West Midlands, B29 6LR

A911YOE	Mercedes-Benz L608D	Patterson	C19F	1984	
C324OFL	Ford Transit 190	Dormobile	B16F	1986	Ex Viscount, 1992
LIW3221	Volvo B10M-61	Caetano Algarve	C53F	1986	Ex Parks, Hamilton, 1990

	Leyland Cub CU435	Reeve Burgess	B20DL	1986	
D314EFK	D318EFK	D692FDH		D695FDH	D698FDH
D315EFK	D319EFK	D693FDH		D696FDH	D699FDH
D316EFK	D691FDH	D694FDH		D697FDH	D700FDH
D317EFK					

LIW3222	Kässbohrer Setra S215HR	Kässbohrer Rational	C53F	1987	Ex Reid, London E1, 1990
D627BCK	Iveco Daily 49.10	Robin Hood City Nippy	B25F	1987	Ex Ribble, 1993
E533UOK	Mercedes-Benz 609D	Reeve Burgess Beaver	C23F	1988	
F370MUT	Dennis Javelin 11SDL1905	Plaxton Paramount 3200 III	C53F	1988	
F906PFH	Leyland Swift LBM6T/2RA	G C Smith Whippet	C33FL	1988	Ex Gloucestershire CC, 1993
G360FOP	Mercedes-Benz 709D	Carlyle	B25F	1989	Ex Tidworth Silver Star, 1991
G395OWB	Mercedes-Benz 811D	Whittaker-Europa	B26F	1990	Ex Globe, Barnsley, 1992
G834RDS	Mercedes-Benz 811D	Reeve Burgess Beaver	B33F	1990	Ex Worthington, Collingham, 1993
H557XNN	Iveco Daily 49.10	Carlyle Dailybus	B25F	1990	Ex Trent, 1993
H741TWB	Mercedes-Benz 709D	Reeve Burgess Beaver	C23F	1991	
H742TWB	Mercedes-Benz 709D	Reeve Burgess Beaver	C23F	1991	
J11OPY	Mercedes-Benz 709D	Reeve Burgess Beaver	C23F	1991	
J221HDS	Mercedes-Benz 709D	Reeve Burgess Beaver	C23F	1992	
K6BUS	Mercedes-Benz 811D	Dormobile Routemaker	B33F	1992	
K7BUS	Mercedes-Benz 811D	Dormobile Routemaker	B33F	1992	
K8BUS	Mercedes-Benz 811D	Wright	B33F	1992	
K578YOJ	Mercedes-Benz 709D	Dormobile Routemaker	B29F	1993	
K579YOJ	Mercedes-Benz 709D	Dormobile Routemaker	B29F	1993	
K580YOJ	Mercedes-Benz 811D	Dormobile Routemaker	B33F	1993	

Previous Registrations:

LIW3221	C705KDS	LIW3222	D397BPE

Livery: Green, white and orange.

Patterson's steadily expanding fleet contains some 15 Mercedes-Benz based minibuses mostly 709D or 811D variants. J221HDS, with Reeve Burgess Beaver bodywork is one of the former.

PETE'S TRAVEL

Pete's Travel Ltd, 40 Sandringham Road, Great Barr, Birmingham, West Midlands, B42 1PH

Depot: 76 Brookside, Great Barr and Unit 52, Queen Court Trading Estate, Greats Green, West Bromwich.

C833CBU	Renault-Dodge S56	Northern Counties	B18F	1986	Ex Patterson, Birmingham, 1993
D138LTA	Renault-Dodge S56	Reeve Burgess	B23F	1986	Ex Cardiff, 1993
D158LTA	Renault-Dodge S56	Reeve Burgess	B23F	1986	Ex Cardiff, 1994
D161LTA	Renault-Dodge S56	Reeve Burgess	B23F	1986	Ex Cardiff, 1994
D175LTA	Renault-Dodge S56	Reeve Burgess	B23F	1986	Ex Plymouth, 1993
D126OWG	Renault-Dodge S56	Reeve Burgess	B25F	1987	Ex Stoniers, Newcastle, 1993
D821RYS	Renault-Dodge S56	Alexander AM	B25F	1987	Ex Sherratt, Cold Meece, 1993

Livery: White

Another recent arrival in the West Midlands area is Pete's Travel who have added variety to their small fleet of Renault-Dodge minibuses by selecting examples from three principal coachbuilders. D126OWG is an example with Reeve Burgess bodywork. *Roy Marshall*

PHILLIPS

I R Phillips, 26 Kempton Avenue, Bobblestock, Hereford & Worcester, HR4 9TU

Depot: Golden Pioneer Coaches, Redhill, Hereford

LUH105P	Bristol LHS6L	Eastern Coach Works	B27F	1976	Ex PCV trainer,1991
DWA707V	Ford R1114	Plaxton Supreme IV	C53F	1979	Ex MY Travel, 1994
MRJ271W	Leyland Leopard PSU5D/4R	Plaxton Supreme IV	C48F	1980	Ex C-Line, 1992
MSL194X	Leyland Tiger TRCTL11/3R	Plaxton Supreme VI	C53F	1982	Ex Moffat& Williamson, 1994
D911MWT	Freight Rover Sherpa	Dormobile	DP20F	1987	Ex Gordon's, Rowley Regis, 1993

Previous Registrations:
MSL194X   MAX335X, FSU372

Livery: White and yellow

Phillips provide local stage services in Hereford and while OJD89R, seen here working the Newton Farm service, has recently been withdrawn, similar bus LUH105P can still be seen. The latest arrival in the fleet is Phillips' first Leyland Tiger which still retains Moffat & Williams livery as we go to press.
Richard Eversden

PRIMROSE

Primrose Motor Services (Leominster) Ltd, Worcester Road, Leominster,
Hereford & Worcester, HR6 8AR

DHR396L	Bedford YRQ	Duple Dominant	C45F	1973	Ex Stockcross Hire, 1988
JDN824N	Bedford YRQ	Plaxton Elite III	C45F	1975	Ex Stockcross Hire, 1988
JHC975P	Bedford YRT	Plaxton Supreme III	C53F	1976	Ex Davie, Rye, 1986
UFO550S	Ford R1114	Plaxton Supreme III Express	C53F	1978	
OFR934T	Bedford YMT	Duple Dominant II	C53F	1979	Ex Stockcross Hire, 1988
AFO245V	Ford R1114	Duple Dominant II	C53F	1979	
DHA986Y	Ford R1115	Plaxton Paramount 3200	C53F	1983	Ex Daisy, Broughton, 1991
IIL1361	Leyland TRCTL11/3R	Plaxton Paramount 3500	C49FT	1983	Ex Summerdale, Letterston, 1992
A416DCN	Bedford YNT	Plaxton Paramount 3200	C53F	1984	Ex Chambers, Prees, 1990
C836CBU	Renault-Dodge S56	Northern Counties	B18F	1986	Ex GM Buses, 1991
F833LCJ	Peugeot-Talbot Pullman	Talbot	B22F	1988	
F834LCJ	Peugeot-Talbot Pullman	Talbot	B22F	1988	

Previous Registrations:

| A416DCN | A264BTY, UPP938 | | IIL1361 | EJV860Y |

Livery: Yellow and white.

The sole Leyland Tiger in the Primrose fleet is IIL1361, an example bodied with a Plaxton Paramount
3500 body. It is seen in its home town of Leominster, though can often be found working the express
service to London which is a regular service provided by this operator. *Bill Potter*

REGENCY MINIBUSES

T J Owen, 5 Comberton Terrace, Kidderminster, Hereford & Worcester, DY10 1QP

F429ENB	Peugeot-Talbot Express	Made-to-Measure	M14	1988

Local services in Leominster are the haunt for the three minibuses in the Primrose fleet. The neat bus station at the edge of Leominster centre is the setting for this photograph of Northern Counties-bodied Renault-Dodge S56 C836CBU, part of the large batch delivered to GM Buses in 1986.
Bill Potter

The double-deck requirement at Regis is met by a pair of Leyland Fleetlines, both new to London Transport and acquired through Partridge of Hadleigh. However, while both were part of the 1976 delivery one is bodied by Park Royal while the other was supplied by MCW. KJD24P and KJD58P are seen ot the Challow Station depot.
Bill Potter

REGIS COACHES

PWJ, JH & N Manning, Challow Station, Stanford-in-the-Vale, Faringdon,
Oxfordshire, SN7 8XY

KJD24P	Leyland Fleetline FE30AGR	MCW	H44/24D	1976	Ex Partridge, Hadleigh, 1991
KJD58P	Leyland Fleetline FE30ALR	Park Royal	H44/24D	1976	Ex Partridge, Hadleigh, 1993
VWY279	Ford R1014	Plaxton Supreme III	C41F	1978	Ex Unique, Brighton, 1985
5212EL	Bedford YMT	Caetano Alpha	C53F	1980	Ex Eagle Line, Swindon, 1985
NNV264V	Mercedes-Benz L307D	Imperial	M12	1980	Ex Private owner, 1985
RJU999W	Bedford YMT	Plaxton Supreme IV	C53F	1980	Ex Walls, Wigan, 1987
YSG653W	Seddon Pennine 7	Alexander AYS	B53F	1980	Ex D & G, Rachub, 1993
JTF972W	Leyland National 2 NL116L11/1R		B52F	1981	Ex Atomic Energy Authority, 1989
E41SBO	Dennis Javelin 11SDA1906	Duple 320	C53F	1988	Ex Bebb, Llantwit Fardre, 1990
G280BEL	Dennis Javelin 12SDA1907	Caetano Algarve	C53F	1989	
G281BEL	Dennis Javelin 12SDA1907	Caetano Algarve	C53F	1989	
G154ELJ	Toyota Coaster HB31R	Caetano Optimo	C18F	1990	

Previous Registrations:

5212EL	DMR675V	VWY279	WLJ213S

Livery: White, blue and red

Regis Coaches operate tendered services in rural south Oxfordshire with destinations of Gloucester,
Swindon and Oxford. To operate the services a Leyland National was added to the fleet in 1989. This
particular bus, JTF972W was new to the Atomic Energy Authority at Harwell for staff use. *Bill Potter*

ROVER

Associated Bus & Coach Investments Ltd, 7 Sherwood Road, Aston Fields, Bromsgrove, Hereford & Worcester, B60 3DR

(A member of Blazefield Holdings group)

152	AYG852S	Bristol VRT/SL3/6LXB	Eastern Coach Works	H43/31F	1977	Ex Harrogate Independant, 1992
359	E359NEG	Volvo B10M-61	Plaxton Paramount 3200 II	C53F	1988	Ex Sovereign Bus & Coach, 1994
360	E360NEG	Volvo B10M-61	Plaxton Paramount 3200 II	C53F	1988	Ex Sovereign Bus & Coach, 1994
364	HIL9374	Leyland Tiger TRCTL11/3R	Plaxton Supreme V Express	C53F	1982	Ex Harrogate & District, 1993
387	YIJ387	Volvo B10M-61	Plaxton Paramount 3200	C53F	1983	Ex Cambridge Coach Services, 1993
392	YXI2747	Volvo B10M-61	Van Hool Alizée	C53F	1985	Ex Shearings, 1990
393	YXI2748	Volvo B10M-61	Plaxton Paramount 3500 III	C49FT	1987	Ex Parks, Hamilton, 1990
394	YXI2749	Volvo B10M-61	Plaxton Paramount 3500 III	C51FT	1988	Ex Bleanch, Hetton-le-Hole, 1992
862	C62LHL	Ford Transit 150	Carlyle	DP20F	1986	Ex Ingfield-Northern Rose, 1994
888	C88AUB	Ford Transit 190	Carlyle	B18F	1985	Ex Ingfield-Northern Rose, 1993

Previous Registrations:

HIL9374	VAV254X	YIJ387	FUA393Y, TXI6342	YXI2748	E568UHS
TXI8762	XWK9X	YXI2747	B490UNB	YXI2749	F885RFP

Livery: Grey and blue

Blazefield Holdings subsidiary, Rover, operates this smartly-presented Bristol VRT, AYG825S. It arrived in 1992 from fellow member Harrogate Independent and is liveried in Blazefield's corporate style. The company have gained much kudos from transport enthusiasts for their warm welcome. *Tim Weatherup*

SANDWELL TRAVEL

J Osborne, Unit 44, Siddons Estate, Howard Street, Hill Top, West Bromwich, West Midlands, B70 0TB

OAF40M	Bedford YRQ	Duple Dominant	C45F	1973	Ex Hambly, Pelynt, 1992
TDF224R	Bedford YRT	Plaxton Supreme III	C53F	1977	Ex Dudley Coachways, 1992
SEL530X	Ford R1014	Wadham Stringer Vanguard	B33F	1981	Ex Dorset Health Authority, 1992
TDC829X	Mercedes-Benz L307D	Devon Conversions	C12F	1982	Ex Alderson-Heil, Wolsingham, 1993
JNO52Y	Ford R1115	Wadham Stringer Vanguard	B42F	1983	Ex Roadmark, Storrington, 1993
SDW236Y	Dennis Lancet SD512	Wadham Stringer Vanguard	DP35F	1983	Ex Redby, Sunderland, 1993
B841WYH	Leyland Cub CU435	Wadham Stringer Vanguard	B32F	1984	Ex LB Islington, 1993
D233MKK	Renault-Dodge S56	East Lancashire	B25F	1986	Ex Boro'line, 1991
D234MKK	Renault-Dodge S56	East Lancashire	B25F	1986	Ex Boro'line, 1991
D235MKK	Renault-Dodge S56	East Lancashire	B25F	1986	Ex Boro'line, 1991
D236MKK	Renault-Dodge S56	East Lancashire	B25F	1986	Ex Boro'line, 1991
D129TFT	Freight Rover Sherpa	Carlyle	B18F	1987	Ex Mountford, Manchester, 1990
D135TFT	Freight Rover Sherpa	Carlyle	B18F	1987	Ex Premier, Dunnington, 1990
D735JUB	Freight Rover Sherpa	Dormobile	B20F	1987	Ex Clearway, Catshill, 1992

Livery: Red and grey

Few major operators have specified the Wadham Stringer Vanguard body, especially on the Ford chassis. The majority that now find their way into smaller operators' fleets will most likely have started life with education authorities or the Ministry of Defence. Sandwell Travel's JNO52Y, was used on airport related work in early life by Ralph's of Langley. *Mike Fowler*

SARGEANT

Sargeant Brothers Ltd, The Nook, Mill Street, Kington, Hereford & Worcester, HR5 3AL

VNT848J	Bedford YRQ	Willowbrook 001	DP45F	1971	Ex Browning, Box, 1986
SGF483L	Bristol RELH6L	Plaxton Elite II	C51F	1974	Ex Davies Bros, Pencader, 1988
CIB9344	Bristol RELH6L	Plaxton Elite III Express	C53F	1974	Ex Steve Stockdale, Selby, 1987
TBD172N	Bedford YRQ	Willowbrook 001	B45F	1974	Ex United Counties, 1982
GRP919N	Bedford YRQ	Willowbrook 001	B45F	1974	Ex United Counties, 1981
KEY212P	Bedford SB5	Willowbrook	B41F	1976	Ex Gypsy Queen, Langley Park, 1991
SJO871T	Bedford YMT(Leyland)	Plaxton Supreme IV Express	C53F	1978	Ex Evans, Tregaron, 1992
AUJ732T	Bedford YMT	Duple Dominant II	C53F	1978	Ex Whittle, Highley, 1982
AVJ900V	Bedford YMT	Plaxton Supreme IV Express	C53F	1979	Ex Yeomans, Hereford, 1985
PUB13W	Bedford YLQ (Leyland)	Plaxton Supreme IV	C45F	1980	Ex Evans, Welshpool, 1992
CIB9321	Bedford YMQ	Plaxton Supreme IV Express	C35F	1980	Ex Munro, Jedburgh, 1991
CIB7615	Bedford YNT	Plaxton Paramount 3200	C53F	1983	Ex Bedford demonstrator, 1988
CIB7866	Leyland Tiger TRCTL11/3R	Plaxton Paramount 3500	C48FT	1983	Ex Midland Fox, 1991
A457PFO	Bedford CF	Dormobile	M12	1984	
D829KWT	Freight Rover Sherpa	Dormobile	B16F	1987	Ex West Riding, 1990
E95RWR	Mercedes-Benz 811D	Optare StarRider	B33F	1987	Ex Northern Bus, Anston, 1989
E168TWO	Freight Rover Sherpa	Carlyle Citybus 2	B20F	1988	Ex H B Transport, Faversham, 1993
F660EDH	Ford Transit VE6	Ford	M11	1988	Acquired 1991
F324BRN	Ford Transit VE6	Ford	M14	1988	Ex Kellor, 1993
H753ELP	Ford Transit VE6	Ford	M11	1990	Ex L W Tours, London N2, 1992
L91WBX	Renault Trafic	Cymric	M16	1993	

Previous Registrations:

CIB7615	KVS655Y	CIB9321	XSH397V	SGF483L	40WMN
CIB7866	ANA109Y	CIB9344	NYG804M		

Livery: Red and gold

Sargents of Kinston are the survivors of a once-extensive business that traversed the English-Welsh border as far west as Llanwrtyd Wells. Operations are now predominantly on the English side of the border and to operate their stage services Optare StarRider E95RWR was added to the fleet in 1989.
David Donati

SMITH'S

Smith's Motors (Ledbury) Ltd, Coach Garage, Homend, Ledbury,
Hereford & Worcester, HR8 1BA

BRH184T	Leyland Leopard PSU3E/4R	Plaxton Supreme IV	C53F	1979	Ex Evans, Tregaron, 1992
OKV399W	Bedford YMT	Plaxton Supreme IV Express	C53F	1980	Ex Evans, Tregaron, 1991
WDG230X	Ford R1114	Duple Dominant IV	C53F	1982	
MVJ721Y	Bedford CF	Dormobile	M12	1983	
GIL1481	Leyland Royal Tiger RT	Plaxton Paramount 3500	C52F	1985	Ex Worthing Coaches, 1990
D124HMT	Leyland Royal Tiger RT	Van Hool Alizée	C53F	1987	Ex Greenslades, Exeter, 1993
D700BJF	Bedford YNV Venturer	Duple 320	C57F	1987	Ex Alpha, Brighton, 1988
D83WWV	Bedford YNV Venturer	Duple 320	C57F	1987	Ex Alpha, Brighton, 1989
J733USF	Mercedes-Benz 811D	PMT Ami	C33F	1991	Ex Fiesta, Hale, 1994

Livery: White, red, green and grey

The small market town of Ledbury has supported two operators, Newbury Coaches and Smiths, for many years. Waiting time in Gloucester bus station is Smiths' D83WWV, one of two Bedford Venturers in the fleet. Its intended destination, Malvern, is shown on a vehicle plate in the front screen.
Richard Eversden

SPRING

WR & GR Spring, 50 Lime Street, Evesham, Hereford & Worcester,

Depot: Hinton Station, Hinton-on-the-Green,

SWP297P	Leyland Leopard PSU3C/4R	Plaxton Supreme III	C53F	1976	Ex Excelsior, Dinnington, 1987
WFS154R	Ford R1114	Plaxton Supreme III	C53F	1977	Ex Collingwood, Wheatley Hill, 1992
DRB60T	Leyland Leopard PSU5C/4R	Plaxton Supreme IV	C57F	1979	Ex Torr, Gedling, 1993
JNJ24V	Leyland Leopard PSU3E/4R	Plaxton Supreme IV Express	C48F	1980	Ex James, Easton Grey, 1993
YUY94W	Ford R1114	Plaxton Supreme IV	C53F	1980	
JNP911X	Ford R1114	Plaxton Supreme V	C53F	1982	
FNM746Y	Ford Transit 190	Chassis Developments	M16	1983	
UAM207	Volvo B10M-61	Duple Laser	C57F	1983	Ex Harrod, Wormegay, 1989
FDZ5347	Volvo B10M-61	Van Hool Alizée	C46FT	1983	Ex Shearings, 1990
A460CRM	Mercedes-Benz L608D	Reeve Burgess	C21F	1984	Ex Waters, Addlestone, 1992
9896EL	Volvo B10M-61	Plaxton Paramount 3500	C49FT	1984	
C125DWR	Volvo B10M-61	Plaxton Paramount 3500 II	C49FT	1986	Ex Wallace Arnold, 1993
E833LNP	Volvo B10M-61	Caetano Algarve	C51FT	1988	

Previous Registrations:

9896EL	A852AUY	SWP297P	PBR954P, 9896EL
FDZ5347	PGC519Y	UAM207	MSU583Y
JNJ24V	GWV927V, 413DCD		

Livery: Cream and red

Oldest vehicle in the fleet of W R Spring & Son is Plaxton Supreme-bodied Leyland Leopard SWP297P. This mark is discerning as, although local, it is a re-registration series. The setting is of Cheltenham bus station in late Autumn where the vehicle awaits time before the return journey to Evesham. *Richard Eversden*

The importation of Ikarus, once the largest bus and coach builder in the world, was effected by stresses of Hungary's economy. Thames Transit have accumulated one of the largest fleets of this marque in the United Kingdom and 23, H917FTT is seen laying-over at the Oxford end of the route. *Phillip Stephenson*

Bearing the original style of Oxford Tube sign writing, Leyland Tiger 11, LSV670, turns into Ecclestone Bridge, Victoria. The intensive nature of the Oxford to London services require some two dozen vehicles. *Colin Lloyd*

THAMES TRANSIT

Thames Transit Ltd, Horspath Road, Cowley, Oxfordshire, OX4 2RY

Depots: Horspath Road, Cowley and Corn Street, Witney.

1	L723JUD	Volvo B10M-60	Jonckheere Deauville P599	C49FT	1994	
2	L724JUD	Volvo B10M-60	Jonckheere Deauville P599	C49FT	1994	

3-7		Volvo B10M-60	Jonckheere Deauville P599	C49FT	1993	

3	L210GJO	4	L211GJO	5	L212GJO	6	L213GJO	7	L214GJO

9	D142PTT	Leyland Tiger TRCTL11/3RH	Plaxton Paramount 3500 III	C51F	1987	
10	PYV277	Leyland Tiger TRCTL11/3RZ	Plaxton Paramount 3500 II	C51F	1986	Ex Devon General, 1987
11	LSV670	Leyland Tiger TRCTL11/3RZ	Plaxton Paramount 3500 II	C51F	1986	Ex Devon General, 1987
15	C922HYA	Leyland Tiger TRCTL11/3RZ	Plaxton Paramount 3200 II	C49FT	1986	Ex Southern National, 1989
16	B896YYD	Leyland Tiger TRCTL11/3RH	Plaxton Paramount 3200	C48FT	1985	Ex Devon General, 1990
17	B894YYD	Leyland Tiger TRCTL11/3RH	Plaxton Paramount 3200	C48FT	1985	Ex Devon General, 1990
18	H69CFJ	Volvo B10M-60	Plaxton Paramount 3200 III	C53F	1990	

19-23		Volvo B10M-60	Ikarus Blue Danube	C49FT	1991	

19	H913FTT	20	H914FTT	21	H915FTT	22	H916FTT	23	H917FTT

24	J499MOD	Volvo B10M-60	Ikarus Blue Danube	C49FT	1992	
25	H914PTG	Volvo B10M-60	Ikarus Blue Danube	C49FT	1991	Ex Hills, Tredegar, 1992
26	H915PTG	Volvo B10M-60	Ikarus Blue Danube	C49FT	1991	Ex Hills, Tredegar, 1992
27	H916PTG	Volvo B10M-60	Ikarus Blue Danube	C49FT	1991	Ex Hills, Tredegar, 1992
28	H917PTG	Volvo B10M-60	Ikarus Blue Danube	C49FT	1991	Ex Hills, Tredegar, 1992

The newer style of logo for Oxford Tube services is displayed here on 7, L214GJO, at Grosvenor Gardens, Victoria. Observant readers will date this scene prior to the cessation of sightseeing services by London Cityrama in late 1993. *Ivor Norman*

Transit Holding's built up a large fleet of Ford Transits in its early days and, indeed many are still performing well beyond expectations. Their limited capacity, however, requires alternatives and Mercedes-Benz 7 and 8 series were early favourites in this role. No.345, F403KOD is a 709D model with Reeve Burgess Beaver bodywork. *Keith Grimes*

29	F23LBW	Volvo B10M-61	Ikarus Blue Danube	C49FT	1989	Ex McLeans, Witney, 1993
30	F24LBW	Volvo B10M-61	Ikarus Blue Danube	C49FT	1989	Ex McLeans, Witney, 1993
31	F337CHE	Volvo B10M-61	Ikarus Blue Danube	C49FT	1989	Ex McLeans, Witney, 1993
50	E829ATT	Mercedes-Benz 709D	Reeve Burgess Beaver	DP25F	1988	Ex Devon General, 1989

100-140   Ford Transit VE6   Mellor   B16F   1986-87

100	D100PTT	109	D109PTT	124	D124PTT	130	D130PTT	137	D137PTT
103	D103PTT	115	D115PTT	126	D126PTT	132	D132PTT	138	D138PTT
104	D104PTT	121	D121PTT	127	D127PTT	133	D133PTT	139	D139PTT
107	D107PTT	122	D122PTT	128	D128PTT	135	D135PTT	140	D140PTT
108	D108PTT	123	D123PTT	129	D129PTT	136	D136PTT		

143	E826ATT	Ford Transit VE6	Mellor	B16F	1988	Ex Docklands Transit, 1990

300-324   Mercedes-Benz 709D   Reeve Burgess Beaver   DP25F   1988   Ex South Midland, 1988

300	E300BWL	305	E305BWL	310	F310EJO	315	F315EJO	320	F320EJO
301	E301BWL	306	E306BWL	311	F311EJO	316	F316EJO	321	F321EJO
302	E302BWL	307	E307BWL	312	F312EJO	317	F317EJO	322	F322EJO
303	E303BWL	308	E308BWL	313	F313EJO	318	F318EJO	323	F323EJO
304	E304BWL	309	E309BWL	314	F314EJO	319	F319EJO	324	F324EJO

325-346   Mercedes-Benz 709D   Reeve Burgess Beaver   B25F   1989

325	F775FDV	328	F765FDV	331	F768FDV	333	F770FDV	345	F403KOD
326	F776FDV	329	F766FDV	332	F769FDV	344	F402KOD	346	F746FDV
327	F764FDV	330	F767FDV						

347-354

Mercedes-Benz 709D — Carlyle — B29F — 1990

347	G947TDV	349	G949TDV	351	G951TDV	353	G843UDV	354	G844UDV
348	G948TDV	350	G950TDV	352	G952TDV				

355-366

Mercedes-Benz 811D — Carlyle — B33F — 1990 — Ex Bayline, 1992/93

355	G831UDV	358	G834UDV	361	G837UDV	363	G839UDV	365	G841UDV
356	G832UDV	359	G835UDV	362	G838UDV	364	G840UDV	366	G842UDV
357	G833UDV	360	G836UDV						

638	D638NOD	Ford Transit 190D	Mellor	B16F	1987
655	D655NOD	Ford Transit 190D	Mellor	B16F	1987

993	F603CET	Leyland Tiger TRBTL11/2RP	Plaxton Derwent II	B54F	1988	Ex Kelvin Central, 1993
994	F604CET	Leyland Tiger TRBTL11/2RP	Plaxton Derwent II	B54F	1988	Ex Kelvin Central, 1993

995-999

Leyland Tiger TRBTL11/2RP — Plaxton Derwent II — B54F — 1988 — Ex Burtons, Brixham, 1989-90

995	F278HOD	996	F279HOD	997	F280HOD	998	F281HOD	999	F282HOD

2000-2028

Iveco TurboDaily 59-12 — Mellor Duet — B26D — 1992/93

2000	K701UTT	2006	K707UTT	2012	K713UTT	2018	K719UTT	2024	K725UTT
2001	K702UTT	2007	K708UTT	2013	K714UTT	2019	K720UTT	2025	K726UTT
2002	K703UTT	2008	K709UTT	2014	K715UTT	2020	K721UTT	2026	K727UTT
2003	K704UTT	2009	K710UTT	2015	K716UTT	2021	K722UTT	2027	K728UTT
2004	K705UTT	2010	K711UTT	2016	K717UTT	2022	K723UTT	2028	K729UTT
2005	K706UTT	2011	K712UTT	2017	K718UTT	2023	K913VDV		

Two of the Mercedes-Benz Minibuses carry liveries for Oxford Tube services. Illustrating the scheme is 321, F321EJO, seen outside one of the many Oxford colleges. *Bill Potter*

The five Burton of Brixham Leyland Tigers were transferred to Oxford in 1989 and 1990 where they provided the whole requirement for full size vehicles, particularly on the service to Bicester. Two, almost identical, vehicles were acquired in 1993 from Kelvin Central to join them and 994, F604CET represents the duo. *Phillip Stephenson*

2029-2072

		Iveco TurboDaily 59-12		Mellor Duet		B26D	1993	Ex Bayline, 1993

2029	K730UTT	2031	K732UTT	2070	K924VDV	2071	K926VDV	2072	K927VDV
2030	K731UTT	2032	K713UDV						

2081	K806WFJ	Iveco TurboDaily 59-12	Mellor Duet	B26D	1993
2082	K633XOD	Iveco TurboDaily 59-12	Mellor Duet	B26D	1993
2083	K816WFJ	Iveco TurboDaily 59-12	Mellor Duet	B26D	1993
2084	K620XOD	Iveco TurboDaily 59-12	Mellor Duet	B26D	1993

3000-3013

		Dennis Dart 9.8SDL3017		Plaxton Pointer		B39D	1994

3000	L703JUD	3003	L706JUD	3006	L709JUD	3009	L712JUD	3012	L705JUD
3001	L704JUD	3004	L707JUD	3007	L710JUD	3010	L713JUD	3013	L706JUD
3002	L705JUD	3005	L708JUD	3008	L711JUD	3011	L714JUD		

Previous Registrations:

LSV670	C129KJO		PYV277	C128KJO

Livery: Blue and grey; Red and grey (Oxford Tube coaches incl 315/24); Grey, black and orange (Blackbird Flyer - 3000-13)

At the height of the mid to late eighties minibus boom few people would have predicted their development. Several column inches have appeared seeking a re-definition to midi-bus, so where does that leave the Dennis Dart with seating around forty, the same as most full-sized buses a few decades ago? *(opposite, above)* The latest arrivals in the Thames Transit fleet are fourteen dual-doored Plaxton Pointer-bodied Dennis Darts in a particularly apt Blackbird Flyer scheme for the service through Cowley to Blackbird Lays district. This particular vehicle is 3003, L712JUD and the service competes with Oxford City Bus as does *(opposite, below)* the X9 Park and Ride service. The vehicles used here are dual-doored minibuses, another variant of the minibus development pioneered by Thames Transit. Representing the type is 2029, K730UTT, seen at the southern end of the route. *Bill Potter*

The South Midland Bus Handbook

THANDI TRAVEL

S Thandi, 74 Regis Heath Road, Rowley Regis, West Midlands, B65 0PB

MBC1 Ltd, 74 Regis Heath Road, Rowley Regis, West Midlands, B65 0PB

Taj Coaches Ltd, 1 The Spinney, Walsall, West Midlands, WS1 4NE

Transol Ltd, 14A Holyhead Road, Handsworth, Birmingham, West Midlands

Walsall Travel Ltd, 57-59 Lower Forster Street, Walsall, West Midlands, WS1 1XA

Depots: 14A Holyhead Road, Handsworth; Rolfe Street, Smethwick and Lower Forster Street, Walsall.

TR	UUF322J	Leyland Leopard PSU3B/4R	Plaxton Elite III	C53F	1971	Ex WJB, Smethwick, 1991
M	WNO554L	Leyland National 1151/1R/0401		B52F	1973	Ex Lawrenson, Haydock, 1993
T	WNO561L	Leyland National 1151/1R/0401		B52F	1973	Ex Brown, Blackburn, 1992
TR	NFN69M	Leyland National 1151/1R		B49F	1974	Ex Arrow, Bristol, 1993
TR	NTC628M	Leyland National 1151/1R		B49F	1974	Ex Coakley, New Stevenston, 1992
TR	OAO564M	Leyland National 1151/1R		B52F	1974	Ex Coakley, New Stevenston, 1992
M	PCN423M	Leyland National 1151/1R		B49F	1974	Ex Hatton, St Helens, 1993
M	GUA824N	Leyland National 11351/1R		B52F	1974	Ex United, 1992
TR	SJG340N	Leyland National 10351/1R		B41F	1974	Ex Wilson, Carnwath, 1992
TR	UAE995N	Leyland National 11351/2R		B44D	1974	Ex Harty, Cosham, 1992
TR	XPD230N	Leyland National 10351/1R		B39F	1974	Ex Lothian Transit, Newtongrange, 1992
TR	GMA404N	Leyland National 1151/1R/SC		DP48F	1975	Ex Blue Lake, Chichester, 1991
TR	GOL416N	Leyland National 11351/1R		B49F	1975	Ex United, 1992
TR	HNB21N	Leyland National 10351/1R		B41F	1975	Ex Gaelicbus, Ballachulish, 1992
TR	HNB23N	Leyland National 10351/1R		B41F	1975	Ex Gaelicbus, Ballachulish, 1992
TR	HJA129N	Leyland National 10351/1R		B41F	1975	Ex Gaelicbus, Ballachulish, 1992
TR	HNE636N	Leyland National 10351/1R		B41F	1975	Ex Gaelicbus, Ballachulish, 1992

Now returned to a more urban environment after a sojourn along the picturesque, if damp, coast between Oban and Fort William, HNE636N is one of a quartet of vehicles Transol received from Gaelicbus of Ballachulish.
D Barber

T	HPF298N	Leyland National 10351/1R/SC		DP39F	1975	Ex Blue Triangle, Bootle, 1993
T	HPF315N	Leyland National 10351/1R/SC		DP39F	1975	Ex United, 1992
TR	KNH501N	Leyland National 11351/1R		DP41F	1975	Ex Luton & District, 1992
TR	WXX615	Volvo B58-56	Plaxton Elite III	C53F	1975	Ex O K, Cardiff, 1990
M	KNV505P	Leyland National 11351/1R		B48F	1976	Ex Battrick & Brown, Blackburn, 1991
M	NFW966P	Leyland National 11351/1R		B49F	1976	Ex United Provincial, Denton, 1992
TR	JOX494P	Leyland National 11351A/1R		B49F	1976	Ex Wilson, Carnwath, 1992
T	NEL126P	Leyland National 11351A/1R		B49F	1976	Ex Wilts & Dorset, 1992
TR	NPK255R	Leyland National 10351A/1R		B41F	1976	Ex South Yorkshire, 1992
T	RJT149R	Leyland National 11351A/1R		B49F	1977	Ex Marchwood, Totton, 1992
T	RJT150R	Leyland National 11351A/1R		B49F	1977	Ex Wilts & Dorset, 1992
TR	VPT945R	Leyland National 11351A/1R		B49F	1977	Ex Traject, Halifax, 1993
TR	CBV782S	Leyland National 11351A/1R		B49F	1978	Ex Portsmouth Transit, 1992
T	CUP669S	Leyland National 11351A/1R		B49F	1978	Ex United, 1992
TR	AAK106T	Leyland National 10351B/1R		B44F	1979	Ex South Yorkshire, 1992
TR	OIA6839	Aüwaerter Neoplan N122/3	Aüwaerter Skyliner	CH52/18CT	1981	Ex Waters, Addlestone, 1992
T	OCN423X	Volvo B10M-61	Duple Dominant IV	C49FT	1982	Ex K Line, London, 1992
TR	A877DUY	Volvo B10M-61	Jonckheere Jubilee P90	CH49/9FT	1983	Ex Coleman, Yeovil, 1992
TR	59WPG	Scania K112TRS	Jonckheere Jubilee P99	CH51/19CT	1985	Ex Arrow, Bristol, 1993
T	C933GAT	Freight Rover Sherpa	Optare	B16F	1986	Ex Den Caney, Birmingham, 1993

Previous Registrations:

A877DUY	A125SNH, RDU4	WXX615	JVW424N
OIA6839	STT602X, 4040SC, LES777X	59WPG	B505GBD

Livery: White, orange, and red.

It should be stressed that the grouping of operators under the Thandi Travel heading is for convenience only and does not represent an official practice. However, a degree of co-operation exists between these operators named above such that recognition is eased by this method. WNO554L of MBC1 is the oldest of some 30 Leyland Nationals in the group. *Mike Fowler*

Two more of the
Leyland Nationals
from the Thandi
group. WNO554L,
above, was new to
Eastern Natioal and
is now in the MBC1
fleet, as seen from
the lettering. It is
seen on service 449
at Queens Square.
Right : The only
series B Leyland
national in the Tandy
Travel group is
AAK106T, originally
with South
Yorkshire. It is seen
with Dudley Castle
as a background.
*Tim Weatherup/Roy
Marshall.*

TRAVEL DE COURCEY

Mike De Courcey Travel Ltd, Rowley Drive, Coventry, West Midlands, CV3 4FG

JHA246L	Leyland Leopard PSU3B/2R	Marshall	DP49F	1973	Ex Excelsior, Telford, 1987
YNA331M	Daimler Fleetline CRG6LXB	Northern Counties	H43/32F	1974	Ex Greater Manchester, 1987
SMU924N	Daimler Fleetline CRL6	Park Royal	H45/32F	1974	Ex Coach Services, Thetford, 1989
OJD129R	Leyland Fleetline FE30AGR	Park Royal	H45/32F	1976	Ex Graham's, Paisley, 1988
KIB6993	Leyland Leopard PSU3D/4R	Willowbrook Crusader (1988)	C50F	1976	Ex Meyric, Magor, 1987
SHE507S	Leyland Fleetline FE30AGR	MCW	O46/29F	1977	Ex London Cityrama, 1993
WFH169S	Leyland Leopard PSU3E/4R	Plaxton Supreme III	C53F	1978	Ex McAndrew, Leamington, 1992
MJI2369	Leyland Leopard PSU3E/4R	Plaxton Supreme III	C53F	1978	Ex Reliance, Gravesend, 1989
MJI2368	Leyland Leopard PSU3E/4R	Plaxton Supreme IV Express	C53F	1978	Ex Brentwood Coaches, 1987
MJI7863	Leyland Leopard PSU5C/4R	Plaxton Supreme IV	C57F	1979	Ex Wessex, 1986
MJI2367	DAF MB200DKL600	Plaxton Supreme IV	C57F	1979	Ex J & L International, Chesham, 1992
HIL8516	Volvo B10M-61	Van Hool Alizée	C49FT	1981	Ex Catteralls, Southam, 1992
MJI2364	Leyland Leopard PSU3E/4R	Duple Dominant II	C53F	1982	Ex Ambassador, 1987
MJI2370	Leyland Tiger TRCTL11/2R	Plaxton Supreme V Express	C53F	1982	Ex Enterprise, Coventry, 1989
PHD713X	Ford R1114	Plaxton Supreme IV	C53F	1982	Ex Jack Hughes, Cleckheaton, 1993
MJI2365	Leyland Tiger TRCTL11/3R	Duple Dominant IV	C55F	1983	Ex Westbus, 1989
MJI2366	Leyland Tiger TRCTL11/3R	Duple Laser	C43FL	1983	Ex Busways, 1993

Swimming bath trips are an essential part of school contracts and provide useful employment for vehicles between the start and end of the school day. Former Greater Manchester Fleetline YNA331M from Mike de Courcey's fleet is seen in Coventry. This example features the curved windscreen of the later models. *Colin Lloyd*

ESU241	Leyland Tiger TRCTL11/3R	Plaxton Paramount 3500	C49FT	1984	Ex Armchair, Brentford, 1991
MJI7861	Leyland Tiger TRCTL11/3R	Plaxton Paramount 3500	C48FT	1984	Ex Lightfoot, Winsford, 1990
MJI7862	Leyland Tiger TRCTL11/3R	Plaxton Paramount 3200	C53F	1984	Ex Northumbria, 1990
55MDT	Leyland Tiger TRCTL11/3R	Plaxton Paramount 3500	C49FT	1984	Ex Ribble, 1988
G219EOA	Freight Rover Sherpa	Carlyle Citybus 2	B20F	1989	Ex Strathclyde, 1992
G35HDW	Freight Rover Sherpa	Carlyle Citybus 2	B20F	1990	Ex Bebb, Llantwit Fardre, 1992
G36HDW	Freight Rover Sherpa	Carlyle Citybus 2	B20F	1990	Ex Bebb, Llantwit Fardre, 1992

Previous Registrations:

55MDT	A130MBA	MJI2367	LBM146V
ESU241	A827PPP	MJI2368	OGR50T
HIL8516	STT605X, XCD108, YDP694X	MJI2369	WFH181S
KIB6993	PJF12R	MJI2370	WBF718X
MJI2364	DBH454X	MJI7861	82LUP, A828MRW
MJI2365	JNM752Y	MJI7862	A69NPP, WSV573, A674DCN
MJI2366	TTN12Y, 552UTE, WCN962Y	MJI7863	FDF264T

Livery:
Park & ride (green and white):   G219EOA, G35HDW, G36HDW.

Travel de Courcey also has vehicles with M J de Courcey names as iseen here on KIB6993, a Willowbrook Crusader-bodied Leyland Leopard seen at Coventry. *Richard Eversden*

VANGUARD

Vanguard Coaches Ltd, Croft Fields, Park Road, Bedworth, Warwickshire, CV21 3HS

(A member of Stagecoach Holdings plc)

2007	4012VC	Leyland Leopard PSU3E/4R	Plaxton Supreme IV Express	C49F	1980	Ex Premier Travel, 1991
2011	FDV820V	Leyland Leopard PSU3E/4R	Willowbrook 003	C49F	1980	Ex Devon General, 1989
2012	FDV822V	Leyland Leopard PSU3E/4R	Willowbrook 003	C49F	1980	Ex Devon General, 1989
2013	LOA838X	Leyland Leopard PSU3F/4R	Willowbrook 003	C49F	1982	Ex Tindall, Low Fell, 1991
2016	YBO16T	Leyland Leopard PSU3E/2R	East Lancashire	B51F	1979	Ex G & G, Leamington, 1993
2018	YBO18T	Leyland Leopard PSU3E/2R	East Lancashire	B51F	1979	Ex G & G, Leamington, 1993
2022	DDM24X	Leyland Leopard PSU3F/4R	Willowbrook 003	C51F	1980	Ex Grimsby-Cleethorpes, 1989
2023	DDM31X	Leyland Leopard PSU3F/4R	Willowbrook 003	C51F	1980	Ex Grimsby-Cleethorpes, 1989
2035	A35XBO	Dennis Lancet SD515	East Lancashire	B47F	1984	Ex National Welsh, 1992
2036	A36XBO	Dennis Lancet SD515	East Lancashire	B47F	1984	Ex National Welsh, 1992
2037	A37XBO	Dennis Lancet SD515	East Lancashire	B47F	1984	Ex National Welsh, 1992
2066	3063VC	Volvo B10M-60	Plaxton Paramount 3500 III	C51F	1990	Ex Wallace Arnold, 1993
2067	9258VC	Volvo B10M-60	Plaxton Paramount 3500 III	C51F	1990	Ex Wallace Arnold, 1993
2074	4828VC	Leyland Tiger TRCTL11/3R	Plaxton Paramount 3500 II	C51F	1985	Ex Sovereign, 1990
2075	9737VC	Leyland Tiger TRCTL11/3R	Plaxton Paramount 3500 II	C51F	1985	Ex Sovereign, 1990
2076	6253VC	Leyland Tiger TRCTL11/3R	Plaxton Paramount 3200 II	C51F	1986	Ex Thames Transit, 1991
2077	6804VC	Leyland Tiger TRCTL11/3R	Plaxton Paramount 3200 II	C51F	1986	Ex Thames Transit, 1991

Repaints into Stagecoach livery are slowly appearing on the former Western Travel fleets, but the majority are still in their former colours. 2808, BVP808V, seen here in Coventry before the December 1993 take-over, displays the blue and white livery used by the Vanguard operation. *Ken Crawley*

2343	C904LEW	Ford Transit 190D	Dormobile	B16F	1985	Ex Red & White, 1993
2344	C53FDV	Ford Transit 190D	Robin Hood	B16F	1986	Ex Red & White, 1993
2345	C102HKG	Ford Transit 190D	Robin Hood	B16F	1986	Ex Red & White, 1993
2346	C105HKG	Ford Transit 190D	Robin Hood	B16F	1986	Ex Red & White, 1993
2347	C345GFJ	Ford Transit 190D	Robin Hood	B16F	1986	Ex Red & White, 1993
2348	C352GFJ	Ford Transit 190D	Robin Hood	B16F	1986	Ex Red & White, 1993
2349	C516BFB	Ford Transit 190D	Carlyle	B16F	1986	Ex Red & White, 1993
2507	XGR728R	Leyland National 11351A/1R (DAF)		B49F	1977	Ex United, 1993
2508	THX155S	Leyland National 10351A/2R		B36D	1978	Ex Scorpio, Harrow, 1991
2509	THX231S	Leyland National 10351A/2R		B36D	1978	Ex London Buses, 1991
2510	CBV780S	Leyland National 11351A/1R		B49F	1978	Ex Thames Transit, 1991
2511	CBV783S	Leyland National 11351A/1R		B49F	1978	Ex Thames Transit, 1991
2512	EMB365S	Leyland National 11351A/1R (Gardner)		B49F	1978	Ex Crosville Wales, 1991
2513	LMA411T	Leyland National 11351A/1R (Gardner)		B49F	1979	Ex Crosville Wales, 1991
2514	LUP901T	Leyland National 11351A/1R (DAF)		B49F*	1979	Ex United, 1993
2808	BVP808V	Leyland National 2 NL116L11/1R		B49F	1980	Ex North Western, 1991
2809	SVV589W	Leyland National 2 NL116L11/1R		B49F	1980	Ex Luton & District, 1991

Previous Registrations:

3063VC	G543LWU	6253VC	YDK917, JPU817, C472CAP	9258VC	G544LWU
4012VC	KUB546V	6804VC	WVT618, C473CAP	9737VC	C212PPE
4828VC	C211PPE				

Livery: Stagecoach white, orange, red and blue replacing blue and white

Photographed in Coventry recently was Vanguard THX246S, a dual-doored Leyland National from London Buses, though two similar vehicles still remain and have been included in the recent numbering of the fleet. *Ken Crawley*

WEST MIDLANDS ROAD CAR

West Midlands Road Car Co Ltd, 15 Shrewley Common, Shrewley,
Warwickshire, CV35 7AR

Depots: Frames Hill Garage, Frames Hill and Durham Ox, Shrewley Common

2308	G216EOA	Freight Rover Sherpa	Carlyle Citybus 2	B20F	1989	Ex Sherratt, Cold Meece, 1992
2309	D453CKV	Freight Rover Sherpa	Rootes	B16F	1986	
2310	D822RYS	Renault-Dodge S56	Alexander AM	B25F	1978	Ex Highland, 1993

Livery: White and blue

West Midlands Road Car have now been operating services in the West Midlands since 1992. Though the numbering system suggests a larger fleet, 2308, G216EOA is seen on the first day of operation of route 677. *Tim Weatherup*

WEST MIDLANDS TRAVEL
CENTRAL COACHWAYS
METROWEST

West Midlands Travel Ltd, 16 Summer Lane, Birmingham, West Midlands, B19 3SD
Central Coachways Ltd, 16 Summer Lane, Birmingham, West Midlands, B19 3SD
Black Country Buses Ltd, Bean Road, Steetley Industrial Estate,
Coseley, West Midlands, WV14 9EE

Depots: Summer Road, Acocks Green; Miller Street, Ashton; Bean Road, Coseley, Liverpool Street, Birmingham; Delph Road, Silver End, Brierley Hill; Dudley Road, Brierley Hill; Wheatley Street, Coventry; Whitmore Street, Hockley; Crossfield Street, Lea Hall; Wellhead Lane, Perry Barr; Ridgeacre Lane, Quinton; Bloxwich Road, Walsall; Washwood Heath Road, Washwood Heath; Oak Lane, West Bromwich; Cleveland Road, Wolverhampton and Yardley Wood Road, Yardley Wood.

514	B514MSO	Ford Transit 190D	Scott	M12	1985	Ex Giles & Gaymer, Coseley, 1993
553	D553NOE	Ford Transit 190D	Carlyle	B18F	1986	
554	D554NOE	Ford Transit 190D	Carlyle	B18F	1986	

565-582

			Renault-Dodge S56		Reeve Burgess	B19F	1986

565	D565NDA	569	D569NDA	574	D574NDA	577	D577NDA	580	D580NDA
566	D566NDA	571	D571NDA	575	D575NDA	578	D578NDA	581	D581NDA
567	D567NDA	572	D572NDA	576	D576NDA	579	D579NDA	582	D582NDA
568	D568NDA	573	D573NDA						

583-596

			Iveco Daily 49.10		Robin Hood City Nippy	B19F	1986

583	D583NDA	586	D586NDA	589	D589NDA	593	D593NDA	595	D595NDA
584	D584NDA	587	D587NDA	591	D591NDA	594	D594NDA	596	D596NDA
585	D585NDA	588	D588NDA	592	D592NDA				

601-620

			MCW MetroRider MF150/3		MCW	B23F	1987

601	D601NOE	605	D605NOE	611	D611NOE	615	D615NOE	618	D618NOE
602	D602NOE	607	D607NOE	612	D612NOE	616	D616NOE	619	D619NOE
603	D603NOE	608	D608NOE	613	D613NOE	617	D617NOE	620	D620NOE
604	D604NOE	609	D609NOE	614	D614NOE				

621-650

			MCW MetroRider MF150/4		MCW	B23F	1987

621	D621NOE	627	D627NOE	633	D633NOE	640	D640NOE	646	D646NOE
622	D622NOE	628	D628NOE	634	D634NOE	641	D641NOE	647	D647NOE
623	D623NOE	629	D629NOE	635	D635NOE	642	D642NOE	648	D648NOE
624	D624NOE	630	D630NOE	636	D636NOE	643	D643NOE	649	D649NOE
625	D625NOE	631	D631NOE	637	D637NOE	644	D644NOE	650	D650NOE
626	D626NOE	632	D632NOE	639	D639NOE	645	D645NOE		

Opposite, top: **The angular lines of the Alexander P type and the larger 'quarter light' windows give a distinct continental flavour to its frontal appearance. That it did not find great favour with British operators is suggested by the considerably more successful PS version. West Midlands Travel's 1059, C59HOM is based on a Volvo Citybus chassis.** *Bill Potter*

Opposite, botton: **Despite withdrawals, West Midlands Travel's Metrobus fleet still exceeds one thousand vehicles by a fair margin. One of the oldest still in service 2046, BOK46V, is a DR102 model like nearly all those supplied to WMPTE.** *Bill Potter*

651-665 — MCW MetroRider MF150/17 — MCW — B23F — 1987

651	E651RVP	654	E654SOL	657	E657RVP	660	E660RVP	663	E663RVP
652	E652RVP	655	E655RVP	658	E658RVP	661	E661RVP	664	E664RVP
653	E653RVP	656	E656RVP	659	E659RVP	662	E662RVP	665	E665RVP

666-685 — MCW MetroRider MF150/113 — MCW — B23F — 1988

666	F666YOG	670	F670YOG	674	F674YOG	678	F678YOG	682	F682YOG
667	F667YOG	671	F671YOG	675	F675YOG	679	F679YOG	683	F683YOG
668	F668YOG	672	F672YOG	676	F676YOG	680	F680YOG	684	F684YOG
669	F669YOG	673	F673YOG	677	F677YOG	681	F681YOG	685	F685YOG

701-720 — Mercedes-Benz 709D — Carlyle — B25F — 1990

701	G701HOP	705	G705HOP	709	G709HOP	713	G713HOP	717	G717HOP
702	G702HOP	706	G706HOP	710	G710HOP	714	G714HOP	718	H718LOX
703	G703HOP	707	G707HOP	711	G711HOP	715	G715HOP	719	H719LOX
704	G704HOP	708	G708HOP	712	G712HOP	716	G716HOP	720	H720LOX

801-805 — Dennis Dart 9SDL3011 — Wright Handy-Bus — B34F — 1991

801	KDZ5801	802	KDZ5802	803	KDZ5803	804	KDZ5804	805	KDZ5805

956	WDA956T	Leyland Fleetline FE30AGR	MCW	B37F	1978

1008-1017 — Leyland National 11351A/1R (DAF) — B50F — 1979

1008	AOL8T	1010	AOL10T	1012	AOL12T	1014	AOL14T	1016	AOL16T
1009	AOL9T	1011	AOL11T	1013	AOL13T	1015	AOL15T	1017	AOL17T

WMT's acquisitive streak started with the Metrowest fleet of Coseley based operators Giles and Gaymer (formerly Dankes). Since the 1993 takeover the Metrowest fleet has been boosted by transfers from the main fleet which, while receiving Metrowest's green and cream livery, retain WMT fleet numbers. 677, F677YOG confirms this. *Tim Weatherup*

1018-1047

Leyland National 2 NL116L11/1R | B50F | 1980 | 1025/33/5/9 are B37D

1018	DOC18V	1024	DOC24V	1030	DOC30V	1036	DOC36V	1042	DOC42V
1019	DOC19V	1025	DOC25V	1031	DOC31V	1037	DOC37V	1043	DOC43V
1020	DOC20V	1026	DOC26V	1032	DOC32V	1038	DOC38V	1044	DOC44V
1021	DOC21V	1027	DOC27V	1033	DOC33V	1039	DOC39V	1045	DOC45V
1022	DOC22V	1028	DOC28V	1034	DOC34V	1040	DOC40V	1046	DOC46V
1023	DOC23V	1029	DOC29V	1035	DOC35V	1041	DOC41V	1047	DOC47V

1048-1052

Leyland National 2 NL106L11/1R | B42F | 1980

1048	DOC48V	1049	DOC49V	1050	DOC50V	1051	DOC51V	1052	DOC52V

| 1053 | B53AOC | Dennis Lancet SDA520 | Duple Dominant | DP23DL | 1985 |
| 1054 | B54AOC | Dennis Lancet SDA520 | Duple Dominant | DP23DL | 1985 |

1055-1060

Volvo Citybus YV31MEC | Alexander P | B50F | 1986

1055	C55HOM	1057	C57HOM	1058	C58HOM	1059	C59HOM	1060	C60HOM
1056	C56HOM								

1061-1066

Leyland Lynx LX1126LXCTFR1 | Leyland | B48F | 1986

1061	C61HOM	1063	C63HOM	1064	C64HOM	1065	C65HOM	1066	C66HOM
1062	C62HOM								

Despite being a very popular size of bus in recent years, the short full-size bus has not been ordered by West Midlands Travel, except for a five Dennis Darts some three years ago. The Wright Handy-bus body has proved a popular choice with several operators, and the first of the WMT batch, 801 KDZ5801, is seen in Walsall when new. *Roy Marshall*

1067-1316 Leyland Lynx LX2R11C15Z4R Leyland B49F 1989

1067	F67DDA	1117	G117EOG	1167	G167EOG	1217	G217EOG	1267	G267EOG
1068	F68DDA	1118	G118EOG	1168	G168EOG	1218	G218EOG	1268	G268EOG
1069	F69DDA	1119	G119EOG	1169	G169EOG	1219	G219EOG	1269	G269EOG
1070	F70DDA	1120	G120EOG	1170	G170EOG	1220	G220EOG	1270	G270EOG
1071	F71DDA	1121	G121EOG	1171	G171EOG	1221	G221EOG	1271	G271EOG
1072	F72DDA	1122	G122EOG	1172	G172EOG	1222	G222EOG	1272	G272EOG
1073	F73DDA	1123	G123EOG	1173	G173EOG	1223	G223EOG	1273	G273EOG
1074	F74DDA	1124	G124EOG	1174	G174EOG	1224	G224EOG	1274	G274EOG
1075	F75DDA	1125	G125EOG	1175	G175EOG	1225	G225EOG	1275	G275EOG
1076	F76DDA	1126	G126EOG	1176	G176EOG	1226	G226EOG	1276	G276EOG
1077	F77DDA	1127	G127EOG	1177	G177EOG	1227	G227EOG	1277	G277EOG
1078	F78DDA	1128	G128EOG	1178	G178EOG	1228	G228EOG	1278	G278EOG
1079	G79EOG	1129	G129EOG	1179	G179EOG	1229	G229EOG	1279	G279EOG
1080	G80EOG	1130	G130EOG	1180	G180EOG	1230	G230EOG	1280	G280EOG
1081	G81EOG	1131	G131EOG	1181	G181EOG	1231	G231EOG	1281	G281EOG
1082	G82EOG	1132	G132EOG	1182	G182EOG	1232	G232EOG	1282	G282EOG
1083	G83EOG	1133	G133EOG	1183	G183EOG	1233	G233EOG	1283	G283EOG
1084	G84EOG	1134	G134EOG	1184	G184EOG	1234	G234EOG	1284	G284EOG
1085	G85EOG	1135	G135EOG	1185	G185EOG	1235	G235EOG	1285	G285EOG
1086	G86EOG	1136	G136EOG	1186	G186EOG	1236	G236EOG	1286	G286EOG
1087	G87EOG	1137	G137EOG	1187	G187EOG	1237	G237EOG	1287	G287EOG
1088	G88EOG	1138	G138EOG	1188	G188EOG	1238	G238EOG	1288	G288EOG
1089	G89EOG	1139	G139EOG	1189	G189EOG	1239	G239EOG	1289	G289EOG
1090	G90EOG	1140	G140EOG	1190	G190EOG	1240	G240EOG	1290	G290EOG
1091	G91EOG	1141	G141EOG	1191	G191EOG	1241	G241EOG	1291	G291EOG
1092	G92EOG	1142	G142EOG	1192	G192EOG	1242	G242EOG	1292	G292EOG
1093	G93EOG	1143	G143EOG	1193	G193EOG	1243	G243EOG	1293	G293EOG
1094	G94EOG	1144	G144EOG	1194	G194EOG	1244	G244EOG	1294	G294EOG
1095	G95EOG	1145	G145EOG	1195	G195EOG	1245	G245EOG	1295	G295EOG
1096	G96EOG	1146	G146EOG	1196	G196EOG	1246	G246EOG	1296	G296EOG
1097	G97EOG	1147	G147EOG	1197	G197EOG	1247	G247EOG	1297	G297EOG
1098	G98EOG	1148	G148EOG	1198	G198EOG	1248	G248EOG	1298	G298EOG
1099	G99EOG	1149	G149EOG	1199	G199EOG	1249	G249EOG	1299	G299EOG
1100	G100EOG	1150	G150EOG	1200	G200EOG	1250	G250EOG	1300	G300EOG
1101	G101EOG	1151	G151EOG	1201	G201EOG	1251	G251EOG	1301	G301EOG
1102	G102EOG	1152	G152EOG	1202	G202EOG	1252	G252EOG	1302	G302EOG
1103	G103EOG	1153	G153EOG	1203	G203EOG	1253	G253EOG	1303	G303EOG
1104	G104EOG	1154	G154EOG	1204	G204EOG	1254	G254EOG	1304	G304EOG
1105	G105EOG	1155	G155EOG	1205	G205EOG	1255	G255EOG	1305	G305EOG
1106	G106EOG	1156	G156EOG	1206	G206EOG	1256	G256EOG	1306	G306EOG
1107	G107EOG	1157	G157EOG	1207	G207EOG	1257	G257EOG	1307	G307EOG
1108	G108EOG	1158	G158EOG	1208	G208EOG	1258	G258EOG	1308	G308EOG
1109	G109EOG	1159	G159EOG	1209	G209EOG	1259	G259EOG	1309	G309EOG
1110	G110EOG	1160	G160EOG	1210	G210EOG	1260	G260EOG	1310	G310EOG
1111	G111EOG	1161	G161EOG	1211	G211EOG	1261	G261EOG	1311	G311EOG
1112	G112EOG	1162	G162EOG	1212	G212EOG	1262	G262EOG	1312	G312EOG
1113	G113EOG	1163	G163EOG	1213	G213EOG	1263	G263EOG	1313	G313EOG
1114	G114EOG	1164	G164EOG	1214	G214EOG	1264	G264EOG	1314	G314EOG
1115	G115EOG	1165	G165EOG	1215	G215EOG	1265	G265EOG	1315	G315EOG
1116	G116EOG	1166	G166EOG	1216	G216EOG	1266	G266EOG	1316	G316EOG

1467-1526 Leyland National 11351/1R B50F 1974

1467	ROK467M	1480	TOE480N	1491	TOE491N	1504	TOE504N	1515	TOE515N
1468	ROK468M	1481	TOE481N	1492	TOE492N	1505	TOE505N	1516	TOE516N
1469	ROK469M	1482	TOE482N	1495	TOE495N	1506	TOE506N	1517	TOE517N
1470	ROK470M	1483	TOE483N	1496	TOE496N	1507	TOE507N	1518	GOK518N
1471	ROK471M	1484	TOE484N	1497	TOE497N	1508	TOE508N	1520	TOE520N
1472	ROK472M	1485	TOE485N	1498	TOE498N	1509	TOE509N	1521	TOE521N
1473	ROK473M	1486	TOE486N	1499	TOE499N	1510	TOE510N	1522	TOE522N
1475	ROK475M	1487	TOE487N	1500	TOE500N	1511	TOE511N	1523	TOE523N
1476	TOE476N	1488	TOE488N	1501	TOE501N	1512	TOE512N	1524	TOE524N
1477	TOE477N	1489	TOE489N	1502	TOE502N	1513	TOE513N	1525	TOE525N
1478	TOE478N	1490	TOE490N	1503	TOE503N	1514	TOE514N	1526	TOE526N
1479	TOE479N								

Quite often vehicles purchased for type-testing are sold once the succesful type have been taken into the fleet, partly because they are no longer a standard vehicle. It is, therefore, interesting to see the Volvo Citybuses supplied in 1986 to West Midlands continue to see operation on the main services from their base at Crossfield Street. Photographed in Dudley, while on route 125, is the first of the batch 1055, C55HOM. *Keith Fowler*

The comparative trials between Volvo Citybus and Leyland Lynx in 1986 led to a large order for the latter. The 250 vehicles were delivered during 1989 and, with the subsequent withdrawal from production of the Lynx it is, presumably, back to the drawing board for future requirements. No.1129, G129EOG, departs from Halesowen bus station on a damp Friday in February 1994. *Keith Grimes*

A large majority of WMTs Leyland Nationals and National 2s have been converted to DAF engines with, mostly,only vehicles in reserve not so far undergoing the change. Several, unlike 1036, DOC36V, have also been transferred to the Metrowest fleet. *Tony Wilson*

One of WMTs Leyland Nationals transferred to the Black Country Buses (Metrowest) fleet was 1490, TOE490N from an intact batch of older Nationals now some 20 years old. *Keith Grimes*

Wolverhampton's industrial heritage forms part of the backdrop to the rebuilt bus station from where DAF-powered Leyland National 1502, TOE502N prepares to depart. *Keith Grimes*

The Metrowest fleet contains some half-dozen former London Buses Leyland Nationals and these continue under the new ownership. These vehicles, of which 1901, THX110S is an example, will be joined within the WMT group by several more from the latest purchase, Stanwell Buses (Westlink). Dudley Castle provides the familiar setting.
Bill Potter

1601	UAE993N	Leyland National 10351/1R	B41F	1975	Ex Giles & Gaymer, Coseley, 1993
1602	GEU359N	Leyland National 11351/2R	B44D	1975	Ex Giles & Gaymer, Coseley, 1993
1603	KHT118P	Leyland National 11351/1R	B49F	1975	Ex Giles & Gaymer, Coseley, 1993
1606	NTC606M	Leyland National 1151/1R/0401	B49F	1974	Ex Giles & Gaymer, Coseley, 1993
1609	NTC609M	Leyland National 1151/1R/0401	B49F	1974	Ex Giles & Gaymer, Coseley, 1993
1612	NTC612M	Leyland National 1151/1R/0401	B49F	1974	Ex Giles & Gaymer, Coseley, 1993
1621	NTC621M	Leyland National 1151/1R/0401	B49F	1974	Ex Giles & Gaymer, Coseley, 1993
1627	NTC627M	Leyland National 1151/1R/0401	B49F	1974	Ex Giles & Gaymer, Coseley, 1993
1630	SKF21T	Leyland National 11351A/1R	B49F	1978	Ex Giles & Gaymer, Coseley, 1993
1631	STJ31T	Leyland National 11351A/1R	B52F	1979	
1634	STJ34T	Leyland National 11351A/1R	B52F	1979	
1640	NTC640M	Leyland National 1151/1R	B49F	1974	Ex Giles & Gaymer, Coseley, 1993
1648	LMB948P	Leyland National 11351/1R	B50F	1975	
1659	SGR559R	Leyland National 11351A/1R	B52F	1976	Ex Giles & Gaymer, Coseley, 1993
1662	LJN622P	Leyland National 11351/1R	B49F	1975	Ex Giles & Gaymer, Coseley, 1993
1664	WNO564L	Leyland National 1151/1R	B52F	1973	Ex Giles & Gaymer, Coseley, 1993
1665	GSX865T	Leyland National 11351A/1R	B52F	1979	Ex Giles & Gaymer, Coseley, 1993
1679	EGB79T	Leyland National 11351A/1R	B52F	1979	Ex Giles & Gaymer, Coseley, 1993
1702	PEV702R	Leyland National 11351A/1R	B49F	1976	Ex Giles & Gaymer, Coseley, 1993
1721	UHG721R	Leyland National 11351A/1R	B49F	1977	Ex Giles & Gaymer, Coseley, 1993
1722	HHA122L	Leyland National 1151/1R/2501	B52F	1973	Ex Giles & Gaymer, Coseley, 1993
1731	VNO731S	Leyland National 11351A/1R	B49F	1977	Ex Giles & Gaymer, Coseley, 1993
1737	UHG737R	Leyland National 11351A/1R	B49F	1977	Ex Giles & Gaymer, Coseley, 1993
1740	PTF740L	Leyland National 1151/1R	B52F	1973	Ex Giles & Gaymer, Coseley, 1993
1742	NAT742A	Leyland National 11351/1R	B52F	1975	
1745	PTF745L	Leyland National 1151/2R	B52F	1973	
1746	PTF746L	Leyland National 1151/2R/0402	B48D	1973	Ex Giles & Gaymer, Coseley, 1993
1757	JTH757P	Leyland National 11351/1R	B52F	1975	
1758	PTF758L	Leyland National 1151/1R	B52F	1973	Ex Giles & Gaymer, Coseley, 1993

1801-1830

Leyland National 11351A/1R		B50F*	1977	1818-30 are DP45F

1801	OOX801R	**1807**	OOX807R	**1811**	OOX811R	**1815**	OOX815R
1802	OOX802R	**1808**	OOX808R	**1812**	OOX812R	**1818**	OOX818R
1804	OOX804R	**1809**	OOX809R	**1813**	OOX813R	**1821**	OOX821R
1805	OOX805R	**1810**	OOX810R	**1814**	OOX814R	**1822**	OOX822R
1806	OOX806R						

1823	OOX823R
1825	OOX825R
1826	OOX826R
1830	OOX830R

1836-1865

Leyland National 11351A/1R		B50F*	1978	*1844/5/7 are B22DL, 1854-65 are DP45F

1836	TVP836S	**1841**	TVP841S	**1845**	TVP845S	**1850**	TVP850S
1837	TVP837S	**1842**	TVP842S	**1846**	TVP846S	**1854**	TVP854S
1838	TVP838S	**1843**	TVP843S	**1847**	TVP847S	**1856**	TVP856S
1839	TVP839S	**1844**	TVP844S	**1848**	TVP848S	**1857**	TVP857S
1840	TVP840S						

1862	TVP862S
1863	TVP863S
1864	TVP864S
1865	TVP865S

1901-1906

Leyland National 10351A/2R		B36D	1978-80	Ex Giles & Gaymer, Coseley, 1993

1901	THX110S	**1903**	THX233S	**1904**	THX267S	**1905**	AYR298T
1902	THX135S						

1906	BYW424V

2001-2074

MCW Metrobus DR102/12	MCW	H43/30F*	1979-80	*2028 is O43/30F

2001	BOK1V	**2016**	BOK16V	**2032**	BOK32V	**2046**	BOK46V
2002	BOK2V	**2017**	BOK17V	**2033**	BOK33V	**2047**	BOK47V
2003	BOK3V	**2018**	BOK18V	**2034**	BOK34V	**2048**	BOK48V
2005	BOK5V	**2019**	BOK19V	**2035**	BOK35V	**2049**	BOK49V
2006	BOK6V	**2020**	BOK20V	**2036**	BOK36V	**2050**	BOK50V
2007	BOK7V	**2021**	BOK21V	**2037**	BOK37V	**2051**	BOK51V
2008	BOK8V	**2022**	BOK22V	**2038**	BOK38V	**2052**	BOK52V
2009	BOK9V	**2023**	BOK23V	**2039**	BOK39V	**2053**	BOK53V
2010	BOK10V	**2025**	BOK25V	**2040**	BOK40V	**2054**	BOK54V
2011	BOK11V	**2026**	BOK26V	**2041**	BOK41V	**2055**	BOK55V
2012	BOK12V	**2027**	BOK27V	**2042**	BOK42V	**2056**	BOK56V
2013	BOK13V	**2028**	BOK28V	**2043**	BOK43V	**2057**	BOK57V
2014	BOK14V	**2030**	BOK30V	**2044**	BOK44V	**2058**	BOK58V
2015	BOK15V	**2031**	BOK31V	**2045**	BOK45V	**2059**	BOK59V

2060	BOK60V
2061	BOK61V
2062	BOK62V
2063	BOK63V
2064	BOK64V
2065	BOK65V
2066	BOK66V
2067	BOK67V
2069	BOK69V
2070	BOK70V
2071	BOK71V
2073	BOK73V
2074	BOK74V

2076-2225 MCW Metrobus DR102/18 MCW H43/30F 1980-81

2076	BOK76V	2105	GOG105W	2135	GOG135W	2167	GOG167W	2196	GOG196W
2077	BOK77V	2106	GOG106W	2137	GOG137W	2168	GOG168W	2197	GOG197W
2078	BOK78V	2107	GOG107W	2138	GOG138W	2169	GOG169W	2198	GOG198W
2079	BOK79V	2108	GOG108W	2139	GOG139W	2170	GOG170W	2199	GOG199W
2080	BOK80V	2109	GOG109W	2140	GOG140W	2171	GOG171W	2200	GOG200W
2081	BOK81V	2110	GOG110W	2141	GOG141W	2172	GOG172W	2201	GOG201W
2082	BOK82V	2111	GOG111W	2142	GOG142W	2173	GOG173W	2202	GOG202W
2083	BOK83V	2112	GOG112W	2143	GOG143W	2174	GOG174W	2203	GOG203W
2084	BOK84V	2113	GOG113W	2144	GOG144W	2175	GOG175W	2204	GOG204W
2085	BOK85V	2114	GOG114W	2145	GOG145W	2176	GOG176W	2205	GOG205W
2086	BOK86V	2115	GOG115W	2146	GOG146W	2177	GOG177W	2206	GOG206W
2087	BOK87V	2116	GOG116W	2147	GOG147W	2178	GOG178W	2207	GOG207W
2088	BOK88V	2117	GOG117W	2148	GOG148W	2179	GOG179W	2208	GOG208W
2089	BOK89V	2118	GOG118W	2149	GOG149W	2180	GOG180W	2209	GOG209W
2090	BOK90V	2119	GOG119W	2150	GOG150W	2181	GOG181W	2210	GOG210W
2091	GOG91W	2120	GOG120W	2151	GOG151W	2182	GOG182W	2211	GOG211W
2092	GOG92W	2121	GOG121W	2152	GOG152W	2183	GOG183W	2212	GOG212W
2093	GOG93W	2123	GOG123W	2153	GOG153W	2184	GOG184W	2213	GOG213W
2094	GOG94W	2124	GOG124W	2155	GOG155W	2185	GOG185W	2214	GOG214W
2095	GOG95W	2125	GOG125W	2156	GOG156W	2186	GOG186W	2215	GOG215W
2096	GOG96W	2126	GOG126W	2157	GOG157W	2187	GOG187W	2216	GOG216W
2097	GOG97W	2127	GOG127W	2158	GOG158W	2188	GOG188W	2217	GOG217W
2098	GOG98W	2128	GOG128W	2159	GOG159W	2189	GOG189W	2218	GOG218W
2099	GOG99W	2129	GOG129W	2161	GOG161W	2190	GOG190W	2219	GOG219W
2100	GOG100W	2130	GOG130W	2162	GOG162W	2191	GOG191W	2220	GOG220W
2101	GOG101W	2131	GOG131W	2163	GOG163W	2192	GOG192W	2221	GOG221W
2102	GOG102W	2132	GOG132W	2164	GOG164W	2193	GOG193W	2222	GOG222W
2103	GOG103W	2133	GOG133W	2165	GOG165W	2194	GOG194W	2224	GOG224W
2104	GOG104W	2134	GOG134W	2166	GOG166W	2195	GOG195W	2225	GOG225W

2153, GOG153W represents the West Midlands standard specification Metrobuses with Gardner 6LXB engine and air breaks. A small batch of DR104 variant with Rolls Royce Eagle engines; 2226-2245, was delivered in 1981 however. *Bill Potter*

2226-2245

MCW Metrobus DR104/8   MCW   H43/30F   1981

2226	GOG226W	2230	GOG230W	2234	GOG234W	2238	GOG238W	2242	GOG242W
2227	GOG227W	2231	GOG231W	2235	GOG235W	2239	GOG239W	2243	GOG243W
2228	GOG228W	2232	GOG232W	2236	GOG236W	2240	GOG240W	2244	GOG244W
2229	GOG229W	2233	GOG233W	2237	GOG237W	2241	GOG241W	2245	GOG245W

2246-2275

MCW Metrobus DR102/18   MCW   H43/30F   1981

2246	GOG246W	2252	GOG252W	2258	GOG258W	2264	GOG264W	2270	GOG270W
2247	GOG247W	2253	GOG253W	2259	GOG259W	2265	GOG265W	2271	GOG271W
2248	GOG248W	2254	GOG254W	2260	GOG260W	2266	GOG266W	2273	GOG273W
2249	GOG249W	2255	GOG255W	2261	GOG261W	2267	GOG267W	2274	GOG274W
2250	GOG250W	2256	GOG256W	2262	GOG262W	2268	GOG268W	2275	GOG275W
2251	GOG251W	2257	GOG257W	2263	GOG263W	2269	GOG269W		

2276-2325

MCW Metrobus DR102/22   MCW   H43/30F   1981

2276	KJW276W	2284	KJW284W	2292	KJW292W	2302	KJW302W	2315	KJW315W
2277	KJW277W	2285	KJW285W	2293	KJW293W	2303	KJW303W	2316	KJW316W
2278	KJW278W	2286	KJW286W	2294	KJW294W	2308	KJW308W	2317	KJW317W
2279	KJW279W	2287	KJW287W	2295	KJW295W	2309	KJW309W	2319	KJW319W
2280	KJW280W	2288	KJW288W	2297	KJW297W	2311	KJW311W	2321	KJW321W
2281	KJW281W	2289	KJW289W	2298	KJW298W	2312	KJW312W	2323	KJW323W
2282	KJW282W	2290	KJW290W	2299	KJW299W	2313	KJW313W	2324	KJW324W
2283	KJW283W	2291	KJW291W	2300	KJW300W	2314	KJW314W	2325	KJW325W

2326-2435

MCW Metrobus DR102/22   MCW   H43/30F   1981-82

2326	LOA326X	2348	LOA348X	2370	LOA370X	2392	LOA392X	2414	LOA414X
2327	LOA327X	2349	LOA349X	2371	LOA371X	2393	LOA393X	2415	LOA415X
2328	LOA328X	2350	LOA350X	2372	LOA372X	2394	LOA394X	2416	LOA416X
2329	LOA329X	2351	LOA351X	2373	LOA373X	2395	LOA395X	2417	LOA417X
2330	LOA330X	2352	LOA352X	2374	LOA374X	2396	LOA396X	2418	LOA418X
2331	LOA331X	2353	LOA353X	2375	LOA375X	2397	LOA397X	2419	LOA419X
2332	LOA332X	2354	LOA354X	2376	LOA376X	2398	LOA398X	2420	LOA420X
2333	LOA333X	2355	LOA355X	2377	LOA377X	2399	LOA399X	2421	LOA421X
2334	LOA334X	2356	LOA356X	2378	LOA378X	2400	LOA400X	2422	LOA422X
2335	LOA335X	2357	LOA357X	2379	LOA379X	2401	LOA401X	2423	LOA423X
2336	LOA336X	2358	LOA358X	2380	LOA380X	2402	LOA402X	2424	LOA424X
2337	LOA337X	2359	LOA359X	2381	LOA381X	2403	LOA403X	2425	LOA425X
2338	LOA338X	2360	LOA360X	2382	LOA382X	2404	LOA404X	2426	LOA426X
2339	LOA339X	2361	LOA361X	2383	LOA383X	2405	LOA405X	2427	LOA427X
2340	LOA340X	2362	LOA362X	2384	LOA384X	2406	LOA406X	2428	LOA428X
2341	LOA341X	2363	LOA363X	2385	LOA385X	2407	LOA407X	2429	LOA429X
2342	LOA342X	2364	LOA364X	2386	LOA386X	2408	LOA408X	2430	LOA430X
2343	LOA343X	2365	LOA365X	2387	LOA387X	2409	LOA409X	2431	LOA431X
2344	LOA344X	2366	LOA366X	2388	LOA388X	2410	LOA410X	2432	LOA432X
2345	LOA345X	2367	LOA367X	2389	LOA389X	2411	LOA411X	2433	LOA433X
2346	LOA346X	2368	LOA368X	2390	LOA390X	2412	LOA412X	2434	LOA434X
2347	LOA347X	2369	LOA369X	2391	LOA391X	2413	LOA413X	2435	LOA435X

2436-2475

MCW Metrobus DR102/27   MCW   H43/30F   1982

2436	NOA436X	2444	NOA444X	2452	NOA452X	2460	NOA460X	2468	NOA468X
2437	NOA437X	2445	NOA445X	2453	NOA453X	2461	NOA461X	2469	NOA469X
2438	NOA438X	2446	NOA446X	2454	NOA454X	2462	NOA462X	2470	NOA470X
2439	NOA439X	2447	NOA447X	2455	NOA455X	2463	NOA463X	2471	NOA471X
2440	NOA440X	2448	NOA448X	2456	NOA456X	2464	NOA464X	2472	NOA472X
2441	NOA441X	2449	NOA449X	2457	NOA457X	2465	NOA465X	2473	NOA473X
2442	NOA442X	2450	NOA450X	2458	NOA458X	2466	NOA466X	2474	NOA474X
2443	NOA443X	2451	NOA451X	2459	NOA459X	2467	NOA467X	2475	NOA475X

2476-2610 — MCW Metrobus DR102/27 — MCW — H43/30F — 1982-83

2476	POG476Y	2503	POG503Y	2530	POG530Y	2557	POG557Y	2584	POG584Y
2477	POG477Y	2504	POG504Y	2531	POG531Y	2558	POG558Y	2585	POG585Y
2478	POG478Y	2505	POG505Y	2532	POG532Y	2559	POG559Y	2586	POG586Y
2479	POG479Y	2506	POG506Y	2533	POG533Y	2560	POG560Y	2587	POG587Y
2480	POG480Y	2507	POG507Y	2534	POG534Y	2561	POG561Y	2588	POG588Y
2481	POG481Y	2508	POG508Y	2535	POG535Y	2562	POG562Y	2589	POG589Y
2482	POG482Y	2509	POG509Y	2536	POG536Y	2563	POG563Y	2590	POG590Y
2483	POG483Y	2510	POG510Y	2537	POG537Y	2564	POG564Y	2591	POG591Y
2484	POG484Y	2511	POG511Y	2538	POG538Y	2565	POG565Y	2592	POG592Y
2485	POG485Y	2512	POG512Y	2539	POG539Y	2566	POG566Y	2593	POG593Y
2486	POG486Y	2513	POG513Y	2540	POG540Y	2567	POG567Y	2594	POG594Y
2487	POG487Y	2514	POG514Y	2541	POG541Y	2568	POG568Y	2595	POG595Y
2488	POG488Y	2515	POG515Y	2542	POG542Y	2569	POG569Y	2596	POG596Y
2489	POG489Y	2516	POG516Y	2543	POG543Y	2570	POG570Y	2597	POG597Y
2490	POG490Y	2517	POG517Y	2544	POG544Y	2571	POG571Y	2598	POG598Y
2491	POG491Y	2518	POG518Y	2545	POG545Y	2572	POG572Y	2599	POG599Y
2492	POG492Y	2519	POG519Y	2546	POG546Y	2573	POG573Y	2600	POG600Y
2493	POG493Y	2520	POG520Y	2547	POG547Y	2574	POG574Y	2601	POG601Y
2494	POG494Y	2521	POG521Y	2548	POG548Y	2575	POG575Y	2602	POG602Y
2495	POG495Y	2522	POG522Y	2549	POG549Y	2576	POG576Y	2603	POG603Y
2496	POG496Y	2523	POG523Y	2550	POG550Y	2577	POG577Y	2604	POG604Y
2497	POG497Y	2524	POG524Y	2551	POG551Y	2578	POG578Y	2605	POG605Y
2498	POG498Y	2525	POG525Y	2552	POG552Y	2579	POG579Y	2606	POG606Y
2499	POG499Y	2526	POG526Y	2553	POG553Y	2580	POG580Y	2607	POG607Y
2500	POG500Y	2527	POG527Y	2554	POG554Y	2581	POG581Y	2608	POG608Y
2501	POG501Y	2528	POG528Y	2555	POG555Y	2582	POG582Y	2609	POG609Y
2502	POG502Y	2529	POG529Y	2556	POG556Y	2583	POG583Y	2610	POG610Y

2611-2667 — MCW Metrobus DR102/27 — MCW — H43/30F — 1983

2611	ROX611Y	2623	ROX623Y	2634	ROX634Y	2645	ROX645Y	2656	ROX656Y
2612	ROX612Y	2624	ROX624Y	2635	ROX635Y	2646	ROX646Y	2657	ROX657Y
2613	ROX613Y	2625	ROX625Y	2636	ROX636Y	2647	ROX647Y	2658	ROX658Y
2614	ROX614Y	2626	ROX626Y	2637	ROX637Y	2648	ROX648Y	2659	ROX659Y
2615	ROX615Y	2627	ROX627Y	2638	ROX638Y	2649	ROX649Y	2660	ROX660Y
2616	ROX616Y	2628	ROX628Y	2639	ROX639Y	2650	ROX650Y	2661	ROX661Y
2617	ROX617Y	2629	ROX629Y	2640	ROX640Y	2651	ROX651Y	2663	ROX663Y
2618	ROX618Y	2630	ROX630Y	2641	ROX641Y	2652	ROX652Y	2664	ROX664Y
2619	ROX619Y	2631	ROX631Y	2642	ROX642Y	2653	ROX653Y	2665	ROX665Y
2620	ROX620Y	2632	ROX632Y	2643	ROX643Y	2654	ROX654Y	2666	ROX666Y
2621	ROX621Y	2633	ROX633Y	2644	ROX644Y	2655	ROX655Y	2667	ROX667Y
2622	ROX622Y								

2668-2735 — MCW Metrobus DR102/27 — MCW — H43/30F — 1983-84

2668	A668UOE	2682	A682UOE	2696	A696UOE	2709	A709UOE	2723	A723UOE
2669	A669UOE	2683	A683UOE	2697	A697UOE	2710	A710UOE	2724	A724UOE
2670	A670UOE	2684	A684UOE	2698	A698UOE	2712	A712UOE	2725	A725UOE
2671	A671UOE	2685	A685UOE	2699	A699UOE	2713	A713UOE	2726	A726UOE
2672	A672UOE	2686	A686UOE	2700	A690UOE	2714	A714UOE	2727	A727UOE
2673	A673UOE	2687	A687UOE	2701	A701UOE	2715	A715UOE	2728	A728UOE
2674	A674UOE	2688	A688UOE	2702	A702UOE	2716	A716UOE	2729	A729UOE
2675	A675UOE	2689	A689UOE	2703	A703UOE	2717	A717UOE	2730	A730UOE
2676	A676UOE	2690	A690UOE	2704	A704UOE	2718	A718UOE	2731	A731UOE
2677	A677UOE	2691	A691UOE	2705	A705UOE	2719	A719UOE	2732	A732UOE
2678	A678UOE	2692	A692UOE	2706	A706UOE	2720	A720UOE	2733	A733UOE
2679	A679UOE	2693	A693UOE	2707	A707UOE	2721	A721UOE	2734	A734UOE
2680	A680UOE	2694	A694UOE	2708	A708UOE	2722	A722UOE	2735	A735UOE
2681	A681UOE	2695	A695UOE						

2736-2772

MCW Metrobus DR102/27   MCW   H43/30F   1984

2736	A736WVP	2744	A744WVP	2752	A752WVP	2759	A759WVP	2766	A766WVP
2737	A737WVP	2745	A745WVP	2753	A753WVP	2760	A760WVP	2767	A767WVP
2738	A738WVP	2746	A746WVP	2754	A754WVP	2761	A761WVP	2768	A768WVP
2739	A739WVP	2747	A747WVP	2755	A755WVP	2762	A762WVP	2769	A769WVP
2740	A740WVP	2748	A748WVP	2756	A756WVP	2763	A763WVP	2770	A770WVP
2741	A741WVP	2749	A749WVP	2757	A757WVP	2764	A764WVP	2771	A771WVP
2742	A742WVP	2750	A750WVP	2758	A758WVP	2765	A765WVP	2772	A772WVP
2743	A743WVP	2751	A751WVP						

2774-2860

MCW Metrobus DR102/27   MCW   H43/30F   1984-85

2774	B774AOC	2792	B792AOC	2810	B810AOP	2827	B827AOP	2844	B844AOP
2775	B775AOC	2793	B793AOC	2811	B811AOP	2828	B828AOP	2845	B845AOP
2776	B776AOC	2794	B794AOC	2812	B812AOP	2829	B829AOP	2846	B846AOP
2777	B777AOC	2795	B795AOC	2813	B813AOP	2830	B830AOP	2847	B847AOP
2778	B778AOC	2796	B796AOC	2814	B814AOP	2831	B831AOP	2848	B848AOP
2779	B779AOC	2797	B797AOP	2815	B815AOP	2832	B832AOP	2849	B849AOP
2780	B780AOC	2798	B798AOP	2816	B816AOP	2833	B833AOP	2850	B850AOP
2781	B781AOC	2799	B799AOP	2817	B817AOP	2834	B834AOP	2851	B851AOP
2782	B782AOC	2800	B800AOP	2818	B818AOP	2835	B835AOP	2852	B852AOP
2783	B783AOC	2801	B801AOP	2819	B819AOP	2836	B836AOP	2853	B853AOP
2784	B784AOC	2802	B802AOP	2820	B820AOP	2837	B837AOP	2854	B854AOP
2785	B785AOC	2803	B803AOP	2821	B821AOP	2838	B838AOP	2855	B855AOP
2786	B786AOC	2804	B804AOP	2822	B822AOP	2839	B839AOP	2856	B856AOP
2787	B787AOC	2805	B805AOP	2823	B823AOP	2840	B840AOP	2857	B857AOP
2788	B788AOC	2806	B806AOP	2824	B824AOP	2841	B841AOP	2858	B858AOP
2789	B789AOC	2807	B807AOP	2825	B825AOP	2842	B842AOP	2859	B859AOP
2790	B790AOC	2808	B808AOP	2826	B826AOP	2843	B843AOP	2860	B860AOP
2791	B791AOC	2809	B809AOP						

2861-2910

MCW Metrobus DR102/48   MCW   H43/30F   1985

2861	B861DOM	2871	B871DOM	2881	B881DOM	2891	C891FON	2901	C901FON
2862	B862DOM	2872	B872DOM	2882	B882DOM	2892	C892FON	2902	C902FON
2863	B863DOM	2873	B873DOM	2883	B883DOM	2893	C893FON	2903	C903FON
2864	B864DOM	2874	B874DOM	2884	B884DOM	2894	C894FON	2904	C904FON
2865	B865DOM	2875	B875DOM	2885	B885DOM	2895	C895FON	2905	C905FON
2866	B866DOM	2876	B876DOM	2886	B886DOM	2896	C896FON	2906	C906FON
2867	B867DOM	2877	B877DOM	2887	C887FON	2897	C897FON	2907	C907FON
2868	B868DOM	2878	B878DOM	2888	C888FON	2898	C898FON	2908	C908FON
2869	B869DOM	2879	B879DOM	2889	C889FON	2899	C899FON	2909	C909FON
2870	B870DOM	2880	B880DOM	2890	C890FON	2900	C900FON	2910	C910FON

2911-2960

MCW Metrobus DR102/59   MCW   DPH43/23F 1986

2911	D911NDA	2921	D921NDA	2931	D931NDA	2941	D941NDA	2951	D951NDA
2912	D912NDA	2922	D922NDA	2932	D932NDA	2942	D942NDA	2952	D952NDA
2913	D913NDA	2923	D923NDA	2933	D933NDA	2943	D943NDA	2953	D953NDA
2914	D914NDA	2924	D924NDA	2934	D934NDA	2944	D944NDA	2954	D954NDA
2915	D915NDA	2925	D925NDA	2935	D935NDA	2945	D945NDA	2955	D955NDA
2916	D916NDA	2926	D926NDA	2936	D936NDA	2946	D946NDA	2956	D956NDA
2917	D917NDA	2927	D927NDA	2937	D937NDA	2947	D947NDA	2957	D957NDA
2918	D918NDA	2928	D928NDA	2938	D938NDA	2948	D948NDA	2958	D958NDA
2919	D919NDA	2929	D929NDA	2939	D939NDA	2949	D949NDA	2959	D959NDA
2920	D920NDA	2930	D930NDA	2940	D940NDA	2950	D950NDA	2960	D960NDA

2961-2974

MCW Metrobus GR133/1   MCW   H43/30F   1984

2961	A101WVP	2964	A104WVP	2967	A107WVP	2970	A110WVP	2973	A113WVP
2962	A102WVP	2965	A105WVP	2968	A108WVP	2971	A111WVP	2974	A114WVP
2963	A103WVP	2966	A106WVP	2969	A109WVP	2972	A112WVP		

A batch of 50 Metrobuses including 2916, D916NDA, was delivered in 1986 fitted with high-back seating. Initially these were in a distinctive livery, but as shown with this recent repaint the vehicles now carry the standard livery. *G Kelland*

MCW Metrobus codes, as with the MetroRider represented the specification of the vehicle with new numbers being allocated when minor changes were made. A 1984 addition to the fleet is 2738, A738WVP seen in Birmingham, *Malc McDonald*

2975-3046   MCW Metrobus DR102/64   MCW   H43/30F   1988-89

2975	E975VUK	2990	F990XOE	3005	F305XOF	3019	F319XOF	3033	F33XOF
2976	E976VUK	2991	F991XOE	3006	F306XOF	3020	F320XOF	3034	F34XOF
2977	E977VUK	2992	F992XOE	3007	F307XOF	3021	F321XOF	3035	F35XOF
2978	E978VUK	2993	F993XOE	3008	F308XOF	3022	F22XOF	3036	F36XOF
2979	E979VUK	2994	F994XOE	3009	F309XOF	3023	F23XOF	3037	F37XOF
2980	E980VUK	2995	F995XOE	3010	F310XOF	3024	F24XOF	3038	F38XOF
2981	E981VUK	2996	F996XOE	3011	F311XOF	3025	F25XOF	3039	F39XOF
2982	E982VUK	2997	F997XOE	3012	F312XOF	3026	F26XOF	3040	F40XOF
2983	E983VUK	2998	F998XOE	3013	F313XOF	3027	F27XOF	3041	F41XOF
2984	E984VUK	2999	F999XOE	3014	F314XOF	3028	F28XOF	3042	F42XOF
2985	E985VUK	3000	F300XOF	3015	F315XOF	3029	F29XOF	3043	F43XOF
2986	E986VUK	3001	F301XOF	3016	F316XOF	3030	F30XOF	3044	F44XOF
2987	E987VUK	3002	F302XOF	3017	F317XOF	3031	F31XOF	3045	F45XOF
2988	E988VUK	3003	F303XOF	3018	F318XOF	3032	F32XOF	3046	F46XOF
2989	E989VUK	3004	F304XOF						

3047-3124   MCW Metrobus DR102/70   MCW   H43/30F   1989-90

3047	F47XOF	3063	F63XOF	3079	F79XOF	3094	F94XOF	3110	G110FJW
3048	F48XOF	3064	F64XOF	3080	F80XOF	3095	F95XOF	3111	G111FJW
3049	F49XOF	3065	F65XOF	3081	F81XOF	3096	F96XOF	3112	G112FJW
3050	F50XOF	3066	F66XOF	3082	F82XOF	3097	F97XOF	3113	G113FJW
3051	F51XOF	3067	F67XOF	3083	F83XOF	3098	F98XOF	3114	G114FJW
3052	F52XOF	3068	F68XOF	3084	F84XOF	3099	F99XOF	3115	G115FJW
3053	F53XOF	3069	F69XOF	3085	F85XOF	3100	F100XOF	3116	G116FJW
3054	F54XOF	3070	F70XOF	3086	F86XOF	3101	F101XOF	3117	G117FJW
3055	F55XOF	3071	F71XOF	3087	F87XOF	3102	F102XOF	3118	G118FJW
3056	F56XOF	3072	F72XOF	3088	F88XOF	3103	F103XOF	3119	G119FJW
3057	F57XOF	3073	F73XOF	3089	F89XOF	3104	G104FJW	3120	G120FJW
3058	F58XOF	3074	F74XOF	3090	F90XOF	3105	G105FJW	3121	G121FJW
3059	F59XOF	3075	F75XOF	3091	F91XOF	3106	G106FJW	3122	G122FJW
3060	F50XOF	3076	F76XOF	3092	F92XOF	3108	G108FJW	3123	G123FJW
3061	F61XOF	3077	F77XOF	3093	F93XOF	3109	G109FJW	3124	G124FJW
3062	F62XOF	3078	F78XOF						

3201-3247   Scania N113DRB   Alexander RH   H47/33F   1990

3201	H201LOM	3210	H210LOM	3221	H221LOM	3231	H231LOM	3239	H239LOM
3202	H202LOM	3211	H211LOM	3223	H223LOM	3232	H232LOM	3241	H241LOM
3203	H203LOM	3212	H212LOM	3224	H224LOM	3233	H233LOM	3242	H242LOM
3204	H204LOM	3215	H215LOM	3225	H225LOM	3234	H234LOM	3243	H243LOM
3206	H206LOM	3217	H217LOM	3226	H226LOM	3235	H235LOM	3244	H244LOM
3207	H207LOM	3218	H218LOM	3227	H227LOM	3236	H236LOM	3245	H245LOM
3208	H208LOM	3219	H219LOM	3228	H228LOM	3237	H237LOM	3246	H246LOM
3209	H209LOM	3220	H220LOM	3229	H229LOM	3238	H238LOM	3247	H247LOM

3867	NOV867G	Daimler Fleetline CRG6LX	Park Royal	O47/22F	1969
4069	YOX69K	Daimler Fleetline CRG6LX	Park Royal	O47/33F	1971

6443-6488   Leyland Fleetline FE30AGR   MCW   H47/33F   1976-77

6443	NOC434R	6471	NOC471R	6474	NOC474R	6477	NOC477R	6488	NOC488R
6444	NOC444R								

6536-6560   Leyland Fleetline FE30AGR   MCW   H47/33F   1977-78

6536	SDA536S	6537	SDA537S	6545	SDA545S	6557	SDA557S	6560	SDA560S

Opposite, top: **Metrowest's UHG721R, now numbered 1721 in the common series, basks in summer sun in view of Dudley castle. It was new to Ribble in 1977, though underwent a major overhaul by that company some ten years later.** *Bill Potter*

Opposite, bottom: **West Midlands Travel's only major purchase of new vehicles since the management buyout was a batch of forty Scanias, bodied by Alexander, in 1990. 3223, H223LOM was photographed on the Maypole service, their normal haunt.** *D Barber*

6600-6628 — Leyland Fleetline FE30AGR — Park Royal — H43/33F — 1976-77

6600	NOC600R	6615	NOC615R	6621	SDA621S	6623	SDA623S	6628	SDA628S
6610	NOC610R	6619	SDA619S						

6630-6690 — Leyland Fleetline FE30AGR — Park Royal — H43/33F — 1977-79

6630	SDA630S	6648	SDA648S	6663	WDA663T	6672	WDA672T	6684	WDA684T
6634	SDA634S	6649	SDA649S	6665	WDA665T	6673	WDA673T	6685	WDA685T
6639	SDA639S	6650	SDA650S	6666	WDA666T	6677	WDA677T	6686	WDA686T
6642	SDA642S	6660	SDA660S	6667	WDA667T	6681	WDA681T	6688	WDA688T
6643	SDA643S	6661	WDA661T	6669	WDA669T	6682	WDA682T	6689	WDA689T
6646	SDA646S	6662	WDA662T	6670	WDA670T	6683	WDA683T	6690	WDA690T

6699-6718 — Leyland Fleetline FE30AGR — MCW — H43/33F — 1978

6699	SDA699S	6709	SDA709S	6712	SDA712S	6714	SDA714S	6718	SDA718S
6703	SDA703S	6710	SDA710S						

6723-6760 — Leyland Fleetline FE30AGR — East Lancashire — H43/33F — 1977-78

6723	NOC723R	6735	NOC735R	6744	NOC744R	6752	SDA752S	6758	SDA758S
6728	NOC728R	6741	NOC741R	6751	SDA751S	6757	SDA757S	6760	SDA760S
6732	NOC732R								

West Midlands Travel have three open-top double deckers, one Metrobus and two Fleetlines. Indeed the latter are the only remaining Daimler-built Fleetlines from a once-large fleet of such vehicles. Seen new New Street is 4069, YOX69K. *G Kelland*

6764-6800 — Leyland Fleetline FE30AGR — MCW — H43/33F — 1978

6764	SDA764S	**6767**	SDA767S	**6772**	SDA772S	**6788**	SDA788S	**6800**	SDA800S

6835	WDA835T	MCW Metrobus DR102/1	MCW	H43/30F 1978

6866-6904 — Leyland Fleetline FE30AGR — MCW — H43/33F — 1978

6866	TVP866S	**6874**	TVP874S	**6881**	TVP881S	**6890**	TVP890S	**6898**	TVP898S
6869	TVP869S	**6875**	TVP875S	**6885**	TVP885S	**6891**	TVP891S	**6901**	TVP901S
6871	TVP871S	**6876**	TVP876S	**6886**	TVP886S	**6895**	TVP895S	**6902**	TVP902S
6872	TVP872S	**6879w**	TVP879S	**6888**	TVP888S	**6897**	TVP897S	**6904**	TVP904S
6873	TVP873S	**6880**	TVP880S	**6889**	TVP889S				

6906-7000 — Leyland Fleetline FE30AGR — MCW — H43/33F — 1978-79

6906	WDA906T	**6925**	WDA925T	**6945**	WDA945T	**6963**	WDA963T	**6983**	WDA983T
6907	WDA907T	**6926**	WDA926T	**6947**	WDA947T	**6964**	WDA964T	**6984**	WDA984T
6909	WDA909T	**6928**	WDA928T	**6949**	WDA949T	**6965**	WDA965T	**6985**	WDA985T
6910	WDA910T	**6929**	WDA929T	**6950**	WDA950T	**6966**	WDA966T	**6986**	WDA986T
6911	WDA911T	**6930**	WDA930T	**6951**	WDA951T	**6967**	WDA967T	**6987**	WDA987T
6912	WDA912T	**6931**	WDA931T	**6952**	WDA952T	**6968**	WDA968T	**6988**	WDA988T
6913	WDA913T	**6932**	WDA932T	**6954**	WDA954T	**6969**	WDA969T	**6989**	WDA989T
6915	WDA915T	**6933**	WDA933T	**6955**	WDA955T	**6970**	WDA970T	**6990**	WDA990T
6916	WDA916T	**6934**	WDA934T	**6956w**	WDA956T	**6971**	WDA971T	**6991**	WDA991T
6918	WDA918T	**6935**	WDA935T	**6957**	WDA957T	**6972**	WDA972T	**6993**	WDA993T
6919	WDA919T	**6938**	WDA938T	**6958**	WDA958T	**6973**	WDA973T	**6995**	WDA995T
6920	WDA920T	**6939**	WDA939T	**6959**	WDA959T	**6976**	WDA976T	**6996**	WDA996T
6922	WDA922T	**6940**	WDA940T	**6960**	WDA960T	**6977**	WDA977T	**6998**	WDA998T
6923	WDA923T	**6941**	WDA941T	**6961**	WDA961T	**6978**	WDA978T	**6999**	WDA999T
6924	WDA924T	**6942**	WDA942T	**6962**	WDA962T	**6982**	WDA982T	**7000**	WDA700T

7007	BOM7V	MCW Metrobus DR104/4	MCW	H43/30F 1979

The Leyland-assembled Fleetlines for West Midlands were bodied by MCW, Park Royal and East Lancashire. Eleven of the latter are still in service including 6728, NOC728R. Several of the Fleetlines are held in reserve along with a large number of other vehicles. A substantial hire fleet is also drawn from this pool and these can be seen throughout the country but are retained in our listing. *G Kelland*

Central Coachways:

Reg	Chassis	Body	Seating	Year	Notes
WLT702	MCW Metroliner DR130/29	MCW	CH47/17DT	1986	Ex London Buses, 1988
245DOC	MCW Metroliner DR130/29	MCW	CH47/17DT	1986	Ex London Buses, 1988
C104DYE	MCW Metroliner DR130/29	MCW	CH47/17DT	1986	Ex London Buses, 1988
JIW3694	Bova FHD12.280	Bova Futura	C49FT	1986	
HDZ8354	Bova FHD12.280	Bova Futura	C49FT	1986	
D932ODA	MCW Metroliner DR140/1	MCW 400GT	CH47/16DT	1986	
JIW3695	Bova FHD12.290	Bova Futura	C53F	1987	
JIW3696	Bova FHD12.290	Bova Futura	C47FT	1987	
E906TOJ	MCW Metroliner DR140/3	MCW 400GT	CH47/16DT	1988	
JIW3697	Bova FHD12.290	Bova Futura	C49FT	1988	Ex Kentish Bus, 1988
JIW3698	Bova FHD12.290	Bova Futura	C49FT	1988	Ex Kentish Bus, 1988
HDZ8349	Bova FHD12.290	Bova Futura	C49FT	1989	
HDZ8350	Bova FHD12.290	Bova Futura	C49FT	1989	
HDZ8351	Bova FHD12.290	Bova Futura	C49FT	1989	
HDZ8352	Bova FHD12.290	Bova Futura	C49FT	1989	Ex Harris, Catshill, 1990
HDZ8353	Bova FHD12.290	Bova Futura	C49FT	1989	Ex Harris, Catshill, 1990
G776HOV	DAF SBR3000DKZ570	Plaxton Paramount 4000 III	CH55/19CT	1990	
G778HOV	DAF SBR3000DKZ570	Plaxton Paramount 4000 III	CH55/19CT	1990	
G543JOG	Bova FHD12.290	Bova Futura	C46FT	1990	
5010CD	Bova FHD12.290	Bova Futura	C32FT	1990	
G545JOG	Bova FHD12.290	Bova Futura	C46FT	1990	
787LOM	Bova FHD12.290	Bova Futura	C40FT	1990	
K2CEN	Volvo B10M-60	Plaxton Expressliner II	C46FT	1993	
K3CEN	Volvo B10M-60	Plaxton Expressliner II	C46FT	1993	
K4CEN	Volvo B10M-60	Plaxton Expressliner II	C46FT	1993	
K5CEN	Volvo B10M-60	Plaxton Expressliner II	C46FT	1993	

Previous Registrations:

245DOC	C102DYE	HDZ8352	F77CUY	JIW3696	E908UOH
5010CD	G544JOG	HDZ8353	F88CUY	JIW3697	A663EMY
787LOM	F907CJW	HDZ8354	C904JOF, 245DOC, C566LOG	JIW3698	A666EMY
HDZ8349	F919BVP	JIW3694	C903JOF	NAT742A	JTH766P
HDZ8350	F920BVP	JIW3695	E907UOH	WLT702	C101DYE
HDZ8351	F921BVP				

Liveries: Blue, silver and red;
Management buyout livery: 2447, 2507/76, 2843/80/8/98, 3000/34/42/4/9/55.
Central Coaches - Blue and gold: 568/72/9/81/3-9/91-6, 1008/11, 1481/3/8, 1505/6/16/20/2/4, 1801-5/7/9-11/3/4/8/30/6/7/9/40/6 and coaches
Metrowest - Green and gold: 514, 608/48/67/77/9/85, 1019/24/30-2/4/8/40/5/7, 1468/85/9/90/2/9, 1601-3/6/9/12/21/7/9/31/4/40/8/59/62/4/5/79, 1702/9/21/2/31/7/40/2/5/6/57/8, 1806/25/6/54/6/62-5, 1901-6.
National Express Rapide: G543/5JOG, K2-5CEN

Central Coachways has recently started operating stage services and has received almost fifty vehicles from the main West Midlands Travel fleet. However, the core coach business continues and a total of seven vehicles are in National Express livery including K5CEN, one of four Plaxton Expressliner 2s which, like the original Expressliner body are only supplied on Volvo chassis. *Colin Lloyd*

Five Metroliners, including a trio new to London Buses, remain in service in the Central Coachways fleet. A London example, WLT702 originally C101DYE, is seen at the southern end of the London Liner service. *Colin Lloyd*

WOODSTONES

Woodstones Coaches Ltd, Arthur Drive, Hoo Farm Industrial Estate, Kidderminster, Hereford & Worcester, DY11 7RA

A607HNF	Ford Transit 190D	Mellor	M16	1983	Ex Smith, Chesham, 1988
D258HFX	Volvo B10M-61	Plaxton Paramount 3200 III	C53F	1987	Ex Excelsior, Bournemouth, 1989
D259HFX	Volvo B10M-61	Plaxton Paramount 3200 III	C53F	1987	Ex Excelsior, Bournemouth, 1989
D575MVR	Volvo B10M-61	Plaxton Paramount 3200 III	C53F	1987	Ex Shearings, 1992
F460WFX	Volvo B10M-60	Plaxton Paramount 3200 III	C53F	1989	Ex Excelsior, Bournemouth, 1992
F466WFX	Volvo B10M-60	Plaxton Paramount 3200 III	C57F	1989	Ex Excelsior, Bournemouth, 1990
G536LWU	Volvo B10M-60	Plaxton Paramount 3200 III	C50F	1990	Ex Wallace Arnold, 1993
G537LWU	Volvo B10M-60	Plaxton Paramount 3200 III	C53F	1990	Ex Wallace Arnold, 1993

Livery: White, red and yellow

Working a Brinton Carpet contract special is Woodstones' G536LWU, one of a pair of former Wallace Arnold coaches added to the fleet during 1993. Based on the Volvo B10M chassis these Plaxton Paramount 3500 bodies are to the mark III design and feature the rear continental door. It is seen in Kidderminster bus station. *Bill Potter*

WORTHS

Worths Motor Services Ltd, The Garage, Enstone, Oxfordshire, OX7 4LQ

Depots: The Garage, Enstone and Burford Road, Chipping Norton.

Reg	Chassis	Body		Year	Notes
OJD401R	Leyland Fleetline FE30AGR	Park Royal	H44/24D	1977	Ex Tappins, Didcot, 1993
KBW322S	AEC Reliance 6U3ZR	Duple Dominant II	C53F	1978	
XKV488S	Ford R1114	Plaxton Supreme III Express	C53F	1978	Ex Pathfinder, Freckleton, 1985
GNF7V	Leyland Titan TNLXB/1RF	Park Royal	H47/26F	1979	Ex Thames Transit, 1989
TDM770V	Volvo B58-61	Duple Dominant II	C57F	1980	Ex Lofty's, Bridge Trafford, 1986
FFC322V	Volvo B58-61	Plaxton Supreme IV	C57F	1980	
FUD322W	Volvo B58-61	Plaxton Supreme IV	C57F	1980	
JWL322W	Volvo B58-61	Plaxton Supreme IV	C57F	1980	
SFH483W	Volvo B58-61	Duple Dominant IV	C57F	1981	Ex Stevens, Bristol, 1991
KYV422X	Leyland Titan TNLXB2RRSp	Leyland	H44/24D	1982	Ex London Buses, 1994
KYV429X	Leyland Titan TNLXB2RRSp	Leyland	H44/24D	1982	Ex London Buses, 1993
SKG406Y	Volvo B10M-61	Plaxton Paramount 3200	C53F	1983	Ex K&P John, Llanharry, 1990
A911LUD	Ford R1015	Reeve Burgess	DP31F	1983	Ex NatWest Bank, Heythrop, 1993
551DJB	Volvo B10M-61	Plaxton Paramount 3500 II	C53F	1986	Ex Wallace Arnold, 1991
774YPG	Volvo B10M-61	Plaxton Paramount 3200 III	C57F	1988	
XSK144	Volvo B10M-61	Plaxton Paramount 3200 III	C57F	1988	
F322MFC	Volvo B10M-61	Plaxton Paramount 3200 III	C57F	1989	
G844VAY	Volvo B10M-60	Duple 320	C57F	1989	Ex Crawford, Neilston, 1992
H443JLJ	Volvo B10M-60	Plaxton Paramount 3200 III	C57F	1990	Ex Bere Regis & District, 1993

Previous Registrations:

551DJB	C121CWR	SFH483W	BUY379W, 7842KR	XSK144	F396HFC
774YPG	F318GWL	WWL439T	HLG202T, 551DJB		

Livery: Blue

Worth's predominantly Volvo-based fleet has recently been joined by some interesting vehicles. Two Leyland Titans from London Buses and a shortened Ford R1115 with Reeve Burgess bodywork. This last vehicle is probably the only Ford PSV chassis (other than Transits or truck-derived A0609s) bodied by Reeve Burgess. Pictured, however, is a fairly standard Plaxton Supreme IV-bodied Volvo B58, JWL322W.
Keith Grimes

YARRANTON

Yarranton Brothers Ltd, Eardiston, Hereford & Worcester, WR15 8JL

Reg	Chassis	Body	Seats	Year	Notes
MSF738P	Bedford YRT	Alexander AYS	B53F	1976	Ex Dean Forest, Joys Green, 1989
WVJ300T	Bedford YMT	Plaxton Supreme IV Express	C53F	1978	Ex Yeomans, Hereford, 1984
EUH573V	Bedford YLQ	Plaxton Supreme IV	C35F	1980	Ex Evans, Tregaron, 1989
HFO547X	Bedford YNT	Duple Dominant	C53F	1982	
ALJ915A	Mercedes-Benz 0303/15R	Mercedes-Benz	C53F	1983	Ex Young, Romsley, 1991
C21KBM	Bedford YNV Venturer	Plaxton Paramount 3200 II	C53F	1986	Ex Bedford demonstrator, 1987
PIB5773	Bova FHD12.280	Bova Futura	C49FT	1986	Ex The Kings Ferry, Gillingham, 1992
D684TPP	Freight Rover Sherpa	Chassis Developments	M16	1987	
E242FJU	Mercedes-Benz 609D	Reeve Burgess	C19F	1987	
E506KNV	Volvo B10M-61	Jonckheere Jubilee P599	C53F	1988	Ex Tellings-Golden Miller, 1992

Previous Registrations:

ALJ915A	PUL81Y	PIB5773	C646YKE

For this edition the Yarranton vehicles have fought shy of the camera, so below is Yeomans Alexander-bodied Dennis Dart. This example is based on the 8.5-metre chassis and features the specification required to satisfy contracts with Hereford & Worcester County Council. It is seen in Hereford working service 117 to Newton Farm.

YEOMANS

Yeomans Canyon Travel Ltd, 21/3 Three Elms Trading Estate, Hereford,
Hereford & Worcester, HR4 9PO

#	Reg	Chassis	Body	Seats	Year	Notes
1	PGR619N	Bedford YRT	Willowbrook 001	B53F	1974	Ex Jolly, South Hylton, 1980
2	VWK8S	Bedford YMT	Plaxton Supreme III	C53F	1978	Ex Freeman, Uffington, 1988
3	C795WVJ	Bedford YNT	Plaxton Paramount 3200 II	C53F	1986	
4	A700OCJ	Bedford YNT	Plaxton Paramount 3200 E	C53F	1983	
5	JVJ439P	Bedford YRQ	Duple Dominant	B50F	1975	
6	KVJ700Y	Bedford YNT	Plaxton Paramount 3200 E	C53F	1982	
7	C858XCJ	Bedford YMP	Plaxton Paramount 3200 II	C45F	1986	
9	J74CVJ	Dennis Dart 8.5SDL3003	Alexander Dash	B30F	1991	
11	FAD442Y	Bedford YNT	Plaxton Paramount 3200	C46F	1983	
12	H554YCJ	Dennis Dart 9SDL3002	Carlyle Dartline	B36F	1991	
14	F702MCJ	Dennis Javelin 12SDA1907	Duple 320	C57F	1989	
15	PTV596X	Bedford YNT	Plaxton Supreme IV Express	C53F	1982	Ex Evans, Tregaron, 1989
16	LUX518P	Bedford YLQ	Duple Dominant	C45F	1976	Ex Owen, Llangollen, 1980
17	B904TCJ	Bedford YNT	Plaxton Paramount 3200 II	C53F	1984	
18	BGR631W	Bedford YMT	Duple Dominant	B55F	1981	Ex Davies Bros, Carmarthen, 1989
19	GHL192L	Bristol VRT/SL2/6LX	Eastern Coach Works	H43/31F	1972	Ex Countryman, Ibstock, 1989
20	G659TCJ	Dennis Javelin 12SDA1912	Plaxton Paramount 3200 III	C49F	1990	
21	FAD257Y	Bedford YNT	Plaxton Paramount 3200	C40FT	1983	
22	YCT502	DAF MB200DKFL600	Caetano Algarve	C48FT	1984	Ex Buchanan, Stretton Sugwas, 1991
23	WUG143S	Bedford YMT	Duple Dominant II	C53F	1978	Ex Buchanan, Stretton Sugwas, 1991
24	PAB911T	Bedford YLQ	Duple Dominant II	C31FT	1979	Ex Buchanan, Stretton Sugwas, 1991
25	BNO698T	Bedford YRT	Duple Dominant II Express	C53F	1979	Ex Buchanan, Stretton Sugwas, 1991

Yeomans Hereford town services are mostly maintained by its two Dennis Darts supplemented by recently acquired Maxeta-bodied Bedford YMQs. The longer of the two Darts, and with a body by Carlyle rather than Alexander, is H554YCJ

26	B700SFO	Bedford VAS5	Plaxton Supreme IV	C29F	1984	
27	PCJ900R	Bedford YLQ	Plaxton Supreme III	C45F	1977	
28	BNO699T	Bedford YRT	Duple Dominant II	C53F	1979	Ex Buchanan, Stretton Sugwas, 1991
29	YXI2755	Bedford YLQ	Duple Dominant	B47F	1978	Ex AEE, Winfrith, 1993
30	CCG550V	Bedford YMT	Duple Dominant	B61F	1980	Ex Yorkshire Rider, 1993
31	YCV834	Volvo B10M-61	Plaxton Paramount 3500 III	C49FT	1988	Ex Flights, Birmingham, 1993
32	PFO300R	Bedford YLQ	Plaxton Supreme III	C45F	1977	
33	NNT522P	Bedford YRT	Willowbrook 001	B60F	1976	Ex Brown, Telford, 1978
34	J158CCJ	Dennis Javelin 12SDA1919	Berkhof Excellence 2000	C53F	1991	
35	WVJ530T	Bedford YLQ	Duple Dominant II Express	C45F	1979	
36	K436GVJ	Renault Master T35D	Cymric	C16F	1992	
37	YLW894X	Bedford YMQ	Lex Maxeta	B35F	1982	Ex R & I, Milton Keynes, 1993
38	YLW895X	Bedford YMQ	Lex Maxeta	B37F	1982	Ex R & I, Milton Keynes, 1993
39	YLW896X	Bedford YMQ	Lex Maxeta	B35F	1982	Ex R & I, Milton Keynes, 1993
40	YLW897X	Bedford YMQ	Lex Maxeta	B37F	1982	Ex R & I, Milton Keynes, 1993
41	HCJ909X	Bedford YNT	Duple Dominant	B63F	1982	
42	A300RCJ	Bedford YNT	Plaxton Paramount 3200	C53F	1984	
43	EVJ300W	Bedford YMT	Plaxton Supreme IV Express	C53F	1981	
44	EFO300W	Bedford YMT	Duple Dominant	B60F	1980	
46	KCJ200Y	Bedford YMQ	Plaxton Supreme V Express	C45F	1982	
47	G212TDV	Volkswagen Microbus	Devon Conversions	M8	1989	
48	G249RTT	Volkswagen Microbus	Devon Conversions	M8	1989	

Previous Registrations:

FAD257Y	LFO400Y, YCV834
FAD442Y	KVJ789Y, YCT502
PAB911T	AUJ742T, WLT642
YCT502	A644WCY, 278TNY, A654XWN
YCV834	E VJW
YLW894X	LCY300X, ULL897, GGK239X, GGK239X
YLW895X	LCY301X, 43FJF, GGK237X, RIB7027
YLW896X	LCY298X, 33LUG, GGK238X, RIB4316
YLW897X	LCY299X, SVO89, GGK236X, RIB7018
YXI2755	YRY988T

Livery: Cream and green with orange on most coaches

A daily express service is operated between Hereford and London and at the Victoria end of the route is 34. J158CCJ, a Berkhof Excellence-bodied Dennis Javelin, represents a change from the many years of purchasing Plaxton or Duple products. This was not entirely pre-determined as this vehicle was a cancelled order. *Colin Lloyd*

Among the very last Bedfords purchased new by Yeomans was this 10-metre YMP with Plaxton Paramount 3200 body. C858XCJ is at home in Hereford City centre. *Richard Eversden*

Several of Yeomans' Bedford service buses have more than 60 seated passengers including 41, HCJ909X, which tops the list with 63. A lot less than that are evident as it travels on the Hereford inner ring road which to construct , the ancient city walls were demolished. *David Donati*

West Midlands Travel have recently taken a majority stake in Smiths Coaches (Shenington) Ltd who trade as Your Bus though the operation is to be maintained as a separate entity. Transfer of several vehicles from WMT was taking place as this book went to press. Nineteen of these Plaxton Derwent-bodied Leyland Tigers in the current fleet. Of the eleven dating from 1990, 151, H151SKU, is seen in Digbeth. *Keith Grimes*

As this book was being finalised Your Bus registered several services in Burton on Trent area for which a new depot was being prepared for April 1994 completion. Initially some nine routes are planned. Your Bus operates one of the largest fleets of Ikarus CitiBus bodied vehicles in the country having acquired several secondhand to add to its own new vehicles of which 58, J58GCX, is an example.

YOUR BUS

Smiths Coaches (Shenington) Ltd, 5 Tything Road, Arden Forest Estate, Alcester, Warwickshire, B49 6EX

(A subsidiary of West Midlands Travel Ltd)

Depots: Tything Road, Arden Forest Estate, Alcester and Webbs Garage, Armscote, Stratford-on-Avon.

2	G215HCP	DAF SB220LC550	Optare Delta	B49F	1990	
3	G216HCP	DAF SB220LC550	Optare Delta	B49F	1990	
4	G217HCP	DAF SB220LC550	Optare Delta	B49F	1990	
5	G218HCP	DAF SB220LC550	Optare Delta	B49F	1990	
6	F372KBW	DAF SB220LC550	Optare Delta	DP49F	1989	Ex DAF demonstrator, 1990

7-14   Leyland Tiger TRBTL11/2RP   Plaxton Derwent II   B54F   1988

| 7 | F335RWK | 9 | F337RWK | 11 | E915NAC | 13 | E917NAC | 14 | E918NAC |
| 8 | F336RWK | 10 | F338RWK | 12 | E916NAC | | | | |

15-19   DAF SB220LC550   Ikarus CitiBus   B50F   1991-92

| 15 | H203TCP | 16 | H516YCX | 17 | H517YCX | 18 | J34GCX | 19 | J37GCX |

20	J24GCX	DAF SB220LC550	Ikarus CitiBus	B50F	1991	Ex Pride of the Road, Royston, 1992
21	J25GCX	DAF SB220LC550	Ikarus CitiBus	B50F	1991	Ex Pride of the Road, Royston, 1992
22	J995GCP	DAF SB220LC550	Ikarus CitiBus	B50F	1991	Ex London Coaches, 1992
23	J996GCP	DAF SB220LC550	Ikarus CitiBus	B50F	1991	Ex Pride of the Road, Royston, 1992
24	J997GCP	DAF SB220LC550	Ikarus CitiBus	B50F	1991	Ex Maidstone, 1992
25	J998GCP	DAF SB220LC550	Ikarus CitiBus	B50F	1991	Ex Pride of the Road, Royston, 1992
28	NSM872R	Bedford YMT	Duple Dominant	C49F	1977	Ex Howick, Hebden, 1988
30	KPO14P	Bedford YRT	Caetano Estoril	C53F	1976	Ex Midland Red South, 1989
31	L540EHD	DAF SB220LC550	Ikarus CitiBus	B50F	1994	
32	L541EHD	DAF SB220LC550	Ikarus CitiBus	B50F	1994	
33	L542EHD	DAF SB220LC550	Ikarus CitiBus	B50F	1994	
34	L543EHD	DAF SB220LC550	Ikarus CitiBus	B50F	1994	
43	CWG703V	Leyland Atlantean AN68/1R	Alexander AL	H45/29D	1980	Ex Camm, Nottingham, 1991
45	GHM869N	Daimler Fleetline CRG6LXB	MCW	H44/24D	1975	Ex London Buses, 1986
46	UNA826S	Leyland Atlantean AN68/1R	Park Royal	H43/32F	1977	Ex GM Buses, 1989

49-54   Volvo B10M-61   Ikarus Blue Danube   C53F*   1991   *53 is C49FT

| 49 | J844RAC | 51 | H407LVC | 52 | H408LVC | 53 | H130MRW | 54 | H131MRW |
| 50 | J845RAC | | | | | | | | |

55	GIL2942	DAF SB2300DKV601	Van Hool Alizée	C51FT	1988	
57	TIA5734	DAF SB2300DKV601	Van Hool Alizée	C51FT	1988	
58	J58GCX	DAF SB220LC550	Ikarus Citi Bus	B50F	1992	
61	DWJ565V	Leyland Atlantean AN68/1R	Roe	H45/29D	1980	Ex South Yorkshire, 1991
62	CWG698V	Leyland Atlantean AN68/1R	Alexander AL	H45/29D	1980	Ex South Yorkshire, 1991
64	CWG751V	Leyland Atlantean AN68/1R	Roe	H45/29D	1980	Ex South Yorkshire, 1991
82	J853TRW	Dennis Dart 9.8SDL....	Plaxton Pointer	B40F	1992	
83	J997UAC	Dennis Dart 9.8SDL....	Plaxton Pointer	B40F	1992	
84	J348GKH	Dennis Dart 9.8SDL3004	Plaxton Pointer	B40F	1991	Ex Plaxton demonstrator, 1992
85	K916FVC	Dennis Dart 9.8SDL3017	Plaxton Pointer	B40F	1992	
86	K917FVC	Dennis Dart 9.8SDL3017	Plaxton Pointer	B40F	1992	
87	K918FVC	Dennis Dart 9.8SDL3017	Plaxton Pointer	B40F	1992	
100	JNA587N	Leyland National 10351/1R		B41F	1975	Ex County, Leicester, 1989

149-159   Volvo B10M-55   Plaxton Derwent II   B55F   1990

149	H149SKU	152	H152SKU	154	H154SKU	156	H156SKU	158	H158SKU
150	H150SKU	153	H153SKU	155	H155SKU	157	H157SKU	159	H159SKU
151	H151SKU								

Previous Registrations:

GIL2942	E355EVH		TIA5734	E357EVH

Livery: Orange, white and brown.

Five former South Yorkshire Leyland Atlanteans are currently owned, two with conventional Roe bodies and three with 'Liverpool-style' bodies built by Alexander. Pictured here is 62, CWG698V.

ISBN 1 897990 05 7
Published by *British Bus Publishing*
The Vyne, 16 St Margarets Drive, Wellington,
Telford, Shropshire, TF1 3PH

Printed by Graphics & Print
Unit A13, Stafford Park 15
Telford, Shropshire, TF3 3BB